DECADES

Brian Eno
in the 1970s

Gary Parsons

sonicbondpublishing.com

Sonicbond Publishing Limited
www.sonicbondpublishing.co.uk
Email: info@sonicbondpublishing.co.uk

First Published in the United Kingdom 2022
First Published in the United States 2022

British Library Cataloguing in Publication Data:
A Catalogue record for this book is available from the British Library

ISBN 978-1-78952-239-6

Typeset in ITC Garamond & ITC Avant Garde
Printed and bound in England

Graphic design and typesetting: Full Moon Media

DECADES

Brian Eno
in the 1970s

Gary Parsons

sonicbondpublishing.com

Would you like to write for Sonicbond Publishing?

At Sonicbond Publishing we are always on the look-out for authors, particularly for our two main series:

On Track. Mixing fact with in depth analysis, the On Track series examines the work of a particular musical artist or group. All genres are considered from easy listening and jazz to 60s soul to 90s pop, via rock and metal.

On Screen. This series looks at the world of film and television. Subjects considered include directors, actors and writers, as well as entire television and film series. As with the On Track series, we balance fact with analysis.

While professional writing experience would, of course, be an advantage the most important qualification is to have real enthusiasm and knowledge of your subject. First-time authors are welcomed, but the ability to write well in English is essential.

Sonicbond Publishing has distribution throughout Europe and North America, and all books are also published in E-book form. Authors will be paid a royalty based on sales of their book.

Further details are available from www.sonicbondpublishing. co.uk. To contact us, complete the contact form there or email info@sonicbondpublishing.co.uk

DECADES | Brian Eno in the 1970s

Contents

Introduction

In a roomful of shouting people, the one who whispers becomes
interesting.
Peter Schmidt, collaborator with Eno on the 'Oblique Strategies' set of
cards.

It was 1972 and my sister Julie, five years older than me, was an avid
viewer of *Top of the Pops*. It was the only 30 minutes of the week that my
parents vacated the TV room. We could sing and dance around the room
without having to put up with the disapproving looks of my mother and
father. We already had different tastes in music; my sister mainly liked the
soul artists that performed but I was already a big fan of The Sweet and
liked David Bowie. On that particular edition, the band Roxy Music made
their first *TOTP* appearance playing their latest 7-inch, 'Virginia Plain'. I
stared at the screen. The musicians looked like they had been beamed
down from another planet, wore lots of make-up, dressed wildly and the
music was so strange to my young ears. Every now and then, the camera
would pan to an alien-looking figure adorned in make-up and playing
his keyboard, wearing a pair of brightly coloured gold gloves; I was
transfixed.

That alien was Brian Peter George St John Le Baptiste de la Salle Eno
(born 1948) a man who traversed most of the 1970s being referred to
just as Eno, and helped transform rock into something more like an
art exhibition, pulling into his orbit such diverse people as painters,
filmmakers and avant-garde composers, introducing the world to 'ambient
music' along the way.

In dealing with Eno during the seventies, a few things need to be
addressed first. Number one is that Eno didn't start his recording career
with Roxy Music until 1972. So, my first chapter discussing the initial two
years of the decade will look at the formation of Roxy before I proceed to
then talk about his recorded output from 1972 onwards.

The second is that Eno, from 1973, worked with a considerable number
of artists. This was mainly as a producer, but occasionally, as on the
Genesis album, *The Lamb Lies Down On Broadway*, where he added
synthesizer or other instruments to tracks.

I will be mentioning some of these albums, but the main focus of the
book are albums that Eno either wrote himself or had a larger part in the
collaboration of the project, including writing credits and performance.

Also, during this period, Eno formed the Obscure label, where he produced such artists as Gavin Bryars, Michael Nyman and The Penguin Café Orchestra. Again, I will mention these records but will not be discussing in any detail as it would take a book twice this length to cover all these releases. The same has to be said of his production duties with Ultravox! and Talking Heads, to name but two of the artists Eno produced during this period of time.

Eno's output was quite dilettante during this period and he moved swiftly from glam rock to funk to progressive rock to Krautrock to ambient, as well as soundtrack work that he undertook. You see that he evolved as a musician and as an artist as he explored all the different possibilities that he can could get away with his record company. He pushed boundaries of what rock music was, even though the musicians he got to work on these pieces came from either pub rock bands, jazz and progressive rock, with the occasional experimental musician thrown in for good measure.

During the 1970s Eno set out his stall of wares that pretty much has served him for the rest of his career so far. As a self-confessed 'non-musician' his work from the period has been a major influence on many other artists over the years. I will discuss his work track by track, including the potential meaning behind some of the lyrics; something Eno was always loath to do during this point in his career. This will include his last vocal recordings made during the 1970s (and for quite a few years after) that take place on the two albums he makes with the German band Cluster.

It's strange to think now that seeing that 'alien' on TV 50 years ago would lead to a lifelong interest in the man and his work and, ultimately, this book.

All releases are on Island Records/Polydor Records unless stated.

Re-Make/Re-Model – The Forming of Roxy Music 1970–71

There is a certain amount of truth in saying that Eno stumbled into his musical career. It is at Ipswich College, studying art in the 1960s, that Eno truly discovered himself. He studied art under controversial maverick educator Roy Ascott who introduced a different way of looking at art, especially devouring the more experimental aspects of it, including the 'mind map' technique that Eno has used throughout his entire career. But it is through his lecturer Tom Phillips that Eno discovered avant-garde classical music, in particular the work of John Cage, who had inadvertently invented ambient music in a piece of piano music called 'In A Landscape' written in the year of Eno's birth (1948). It was mainly the American minimalist movement of composers such as Terry Riley and La Monte Young that initially got Eno interested in creating music. This and his meeting with the British teacher in experimental composition, Cornelius Cardew. It was at this point that Eno began to collect old reel-to-reel tape recorders and then slowly pieced together experimental musique concrète. David Sheppard described his first tape compositions in his 2008 book *On Some Faraway Beach: The Life And Times Of Brian Eno*:

> His first recorded 'piece' was the sound of a pen striking the hood of a large anglepoise lamp, multi-tracked at different speeds to form a shimmering, bell-like cloud of tones, over which a friend read a poem. Its hazy reverberations, Eno told me, 'sounded very similar to the music I make now'.

In 1966 Eno entered Winchester School of Art and it is here that he slowly transformed himself into the person who bursts onto the music scene with Roxy Music. It is here that Eno began to slowly discard more traditional forms of painting in favour of sound painting using his collection of tape recorders.

It was also during this period that Eno discovered the New York band The Velvet Underground, who would have a profound influence on his rock career throughout the seventies. At this point, Eno became a performer with the Scratch Orchestra, mainly focusing on works by La Monte Young. Later he started to perform solo concerts with renditions of his own compositions of his manipulated tape pieces as well as piano works by Toru Takemitsu. It was at one of these concerts at Reading University in 1968 that Eno made the acquaintance of Andy Mackay and the pair struck up a friendship, even forming a mostly theoretical band called Brian Iron and The Crowbars. But it was Eno's next band that set him firmly on a course for blending rock music with the avant-garde, with fellow Winchester student Anthony Grafton on guitar and Eno on vocals and signal generator. They mixed blues and Stockhausen electronics and called themselves Maxwell Demon (inspired by Eno, Maxwell Demon was the name given to the character in Todd Haynes' 1998 film about glam rock called *Velvet Goldmine*. The soundtrack also featured songs by Eno). It was also at this point that Eno invested in his first electric guitar called a Starway, which cost him nine pounds and he would use it on a vast number of his recordings during the seventies.

In June 1969, Eno graduated from Winchester with a fine art diploma and a major interest in both modern classical and rock music. Rather than take on the guise of most avant-garde composers, Eno's dress sense became more and more flamboyant, releasing his inner peacock to the world and starting a transformation that would reach its peak in 1973. Eno then relocated to London to indulge in the bohemian lifestyle that was flooding out of the city in 1969. It was a time of experimental rock where Pink Floyd had performed a live soundtrack to the moon landings that summer and radical new bands had emerged from the Ladbroke Grove area, some like Quintessence mixing Western rock with Eastern music and philosophy. It was also the year that Beckenham-based David Bowie scored his first hit single with 'Space Oddity'. Brian scraped a living by being involved with several art ventures and living in one room in a shared house in Grove Park. It was while living here that he began to pick up discarded instruments and electrical goods, including a PA system that once belonged to the cinema advert company Pearl & Dean. It was also during this time that Eno claimed that he starred in pornographic films to make ends meet, although none of these performances have ever come to light.

In 1970 Eno had another musical epiphany when he attended a Philip Glass concert at The Royal College of Art. Glass's repetitive and sombre arpeggiations were a bolt from the blue for Eno and he would later find a way of referencing them in his own music. But Eno was already finding his feet on the classical music stage by performing with Gavin Bryars' Portsmouth Sinfonia, a collection of non-musicians who attempted to play well-known classical standards such as the *William Tell Overture* and, for the most part, failed miserably to achieve this. Eno was playing oboe, an instrument he had never touched before and stood out among the other members of the orchestra with his feminine and dandy appearance giving him a rather androgenous look among the more staid-looking members. Among the other members of the orchestra were Michael Nyman and Simon Fisher Turner.

Eno was still an enthusiastic dilettante and an amateur performer in music at this point until one fateful day, while waiting for a Bakerloo train at Elephant and Castle, he ended up sitting on the train opposite his old friend Andy Mackay. Mackay asked Eno if he 'still had some tape recorders' as he was in a band and they wanted to get some proper demos made. He replied that he did and was willing to record the band, and this is how he entered the world of Bryan Ferry and what was to become known as Roxy Music.

Mackay then told Ferry about his friend with the sci-fi surname and Ferry was so intrigued by Eno's CV within avant-garde music that he invited Eno to his flat to record some of the songs he had written. In early 1971 Eno joined Ferry, Mackay and bass player Graham Simpson to record Ferry's embryonic songs. Eno was impressed with Ferry's songs and felt that he had found something truly original, especially when Mackay's saxophone entered the situation. Mackay was also the owner of a VCS3 synthesizer that also piqued Eno's interest. Mackay had barely touched the instrument, but it would become the thing that Eno would be renowned for in the seventies. Mackay encouraged Eno to take the instrument home with him to explore it further. He plugged it through his PA and then fed it into his tape recorders, where he wobbled and manipulated the sounds that the synthesizer generated; finally the self-professed non-musician had found the tool he could work with within a rock band set-up.

Eno began soundproofing a large second-floor landing at Grove Park, where he set up his PA. This gave the band their first rehearsal space where they could begin to play using a louder volume. It was lucky that his housemates were tolerant of the noises being made by the band. It was here that the band started to audition for drummers and after a few non-starters, they finally found Paul Thompson after Ferry placed an ad in the *Melody Maker* for: 'Wonder drummer required for avant rock group'. All they needed next was the right guitarist. Eno managed to capture on tape some of the first rehearsals with Thompson as the songs began to sound stronger and stronger as new arrangements of Ferry's material took shape. Ferry touted some of these demos around to the music publishers in London's Tin Pan Alley in the vicinity of Denmark Street, but he got turned down by most of them and was told that the songs were just 'too weird'. In truth, bands like Roxy would normally garner interest from playing the live circuit up and down the country, but at this point, the band were far from ready to embark upon playing in front of an audience.

The band continued to rehearse three or four times a week and slowly, his proficiency with the VCS3 improved and his role in the group slowly changed to being a 'sound manipulator' as he began to feed various instruments and even Ferry's voice through the synthesizer. By the time the band started doing live performances, Eno's set-up was his VCS3, two Revox reel-to-reel tape machines, a Ferrograph tape recorder, a control keyboard and a customised echo unit; there was a touch of Heath Robinson in regard to the set-up which all added to its strangeness by Eno's unique sartorial style.

It was at this time that Ferry enlisted ex-Nice guitarist David O'List to the ranks of Roxy, and with O'List's name added to the line-up, Roxy suddenly started to become a newsworthy act within the music press. O'List soon set about streamlining Roxy's song arrangements and even got the band to rehearse some of his songs. Although his tenure in the band was short-lived, O'List features on a John Peel session from 4 January 1972, which finally had an official release in 2018 on the debut album's super deluxe box set. In August of 1971, Roxy got their first interview in the *Melody Maker* paper courtesy of Richard Williams. This interview was conducted solely because Williams had heard a demo tape Ferry had sent, as so far, the band were making headlines but had not yet had an official release or had even played live. Ferry had also sent a demo tape to King Crimson's EG Management and at this point, they were keen to sign the band, hearing something different in their sound (as a management company, they would become very important to Eno's post-Roxy career).

Before the Peel session, the band played a discreet gig at Peel's Perfumed Garden club in London, supporting Genesis. In his 1998 book *Unknown Pleasures* Paul Stump quotes engineer Bill Anthony about the session:

> Despite the strange lashed-up control room, the band seemed happy with the session. I remember Eno asking us about phasing effects machines. He was really into gadgets, and the only way then to get good flanging or phasing effect was to play back two recordings of the sound you wanted to phase off separate tape recorders and knock one slightly

out of phase with the other by rubbing your finger against the flange of the tape reel.

Here we see Eno's fledgling interest in recording techniques that would engulf him as not only a writer and performer but also as a producer and the person who probably spent more time in a recording studio than at home in the seventies.

Most of the tracks were songs that would end up on the first album, such as 'Re-Make/Re-Model', 'If There Is Something' and 'Sea Breezes'. Like later sessions Eno recorded in May of 1972, Eno's synth is to the fore even more so than the album versions recorded a couple of months later. Reactions to the broadcast – on 21 January – were very favourable and led to Peel inviting the band back for another session in May of that year.

Problems were, however, brewing with guitarist O'List's rather eccentric behaviour and his drug use. Also, his musical style was slowly becoming at odds with Roxy's new arrangements and Ferry was growing tired of O'List demanding solos in each song. All these things came to a head at an audition concert in Wandsworth for EG Management, where O'List and Thompson had a stand-up fist fight. Thompson said of this in a December 1995 issue of *Mojo* magazine:

> He never wanted me in the band anyway, so a few punches were thrown or not, O'List was retained on sufferance for a short while longer and then, his behaviour and reliability unimproved, he was sacked and Manzanera asked to join officially as guitarist.

Manzanera was at this point, a part-time roadie and was asked to join initially as a sound engineer. When he objected because he said he knew nothing about sound engineering, Ferry said, 'Don't worry, Eno'll show you how.' In fact, this was a ruse to secretly get Manzanera to play guitar in the band, so he learned all the stuff so that he could play it all first time during his 'fake' audition. He was four years younger than the other members of the band, but Eno took him under his wing and helped ease him into the group dynamics.

It wasn't all plain sailing at first with EG Management, as they initially wanted Ferry to drop the rest of the band and told him they would make him a star. Ferry, of course, baulked at this idea. One of EG's bosses, David Enthoven, wasn't immediately sold on the band but slowly came around and became their greatest ally. He decided to sell Roxy to another young company much like his – Island Records, a label that only a few months earlier had turned down Ferry and his demos. This time Dave Betteridge, Island's marketing chief, liked what he heard and loved the image that the band was now projecting. The rest of Island's management were not so convinced, even some calling the demo 'dreadful', however, company chairman Chris Blackwell kept quiet about his reaction to the music. The next day Enthoven visited Island's offices with planned cover artwork for the album designed by Ferry. Blackwell took one look at the artwork and turned to Tim Clark, one of Island's PR personnel and said eagerly, 'Got them signed yet?'

Here's Looking At You Kid: The First Roxy Music album 1972

By early 1972 Eno had graduated from being Roxy's sound man, standing behind the monitor in venues but filtering instruments through his VCS3, to fully glamorous onstage peacock in front of his keyboard on the opposite side of the stage to Ferry. With Manzanera in the band, the core of Roxy was now complete, and all they had to do was live up to the hype that was being slowly generated about them.

In 1972, glam rock hit big time, Bowie took the UK by storm with his androgenous Ziggy Stardust and The Sweet pelted out some foot-stomping Top 10 hits that kept the glam kids on the dance floor. Roxy was a strange beast that kind of fitted in between the two but also were something unique on their own.

They were more art house glamorous than Bowie's fallen rock star, and Roxy felt almost jet-set with a heavy use of eyeliner. Eno in leopard print and gold gloves with heavy make-up and long hair, looked like he had been lifted from a Weimar-era cabaret performance via the set of *Star Trek*. All of Roxy's outrageous style would be on display on the inside gatefold sleeve of their first album, but first, they had to record it.

Eno discussed the bands 'glam' image in an interview with Steve Peacock in *Sounds* on July 1 1972:

I don't think we'll ever have a smooth, coherent image because we'll always be moving, and there'll always be rough edges to what we do. There's an immediate contrast between what we wear too and what we play – something very incongruous about it. I love that, and I don't think it's a very bad thing to confuse people.

In March of 1972, the band headed into Command Studios in Piccadilly, London, to begin work on their debut album. All was not plain sailing, though, as the budget to record the band was only £5,000, hardly a king's ransom to record a whole album even in 1972. Producer Pete Sinfield (recently fired from King Crimson) did it unpaid but for a 1.5 per cent royalty stake if the album was a success; the problem was Sinfield had never produced before. The album would be recorded in a mere 19 days in what was really a run-down old theatre more than a proper recording studio.

Roxy Music (1972)

Personnel:
Bryan Ferry: vocals, piano
Graham Simpson: bass
Andrew Mackay: oboe, saxophone
Eno: synthesizer, tapes
Paul Thompson: drums
Phil Manzanera: guitar
All songs written by Bryan Ferry
Produced by: Pete Sinfield
Recorded at: Command Studios, London, March 1972
Released: 16 June 1972
Highest Chart Position: UK: 10
Tracklisting: Side One: 1. Re-Make/Re-Model, 2. Ladytron, 3. If There Is
Something, 4. 2.H.B., Side Two: 1. The Bob (Medley), 2. Chance Meeting. 3.
Would You Believe?, 4. Sea Breezes, 5. Bitters End

Before we begin to discuss the music, I must mention the now-iconic
cover designed by Bryan Ferry. Barry Lazell and Dafydd Rees, in their 1982
book *Bryan Ferry & Roxy Music* discuss this:

> Bryan's chosen design was spot on; a deluxe version of a 1950s pin-
> up, glamour pic. The pose and appearance of a model named Kari-ann
> became the focal point of the desired image and no expense was spared.
> For the pose to have impact it required a gatefold sleeve to accommodate
> the reclining figure, an almost unheard-of commodity for a new band
> with unproven sales potential. As a further essential ingredient of its
> glossy image, it was agreed that the sleeve should be laminated.

Even by 1972's standards, we are talking about the height of progressive
rock and some of the most ostentatious artwork ever for rock albums. The
first Roxy cover stood out by being retro, cool and kind of futuristic all at
the same time; there was something chic about Roxy that set them apart
from most other rock bands.

Even the opening track of 'Re-Make/Re-Model' started with the sound
of a party in full flow before Ferry's piano began to hit its power chords
and the rest of the band clattered into the proceedings. This seemed like a
statement of intent – Roxy were brash, melodic and downright weird as if
the party they were playing at was happening on Mars. Ferry's vocals were

a slice of angular wonder, even though producer Sinfield had his doubts about Ferry as a frontman. Eno's vocals can be heard clearly in the song's 'CPL5938' car number plate referencing hook line and his synth wobbled over the track sweeping up and down in an atonal fashion. This was most evident in the band's instrumental breaks near the end of the song, where Manzanera referenced 'C'mon Everybody' and Mackay a touch of Wagner's *Ride of the Valkyries*. It was as though it was Eno's synth bleeps that set the track firmly in the future and also ended the song with a deep bass noise that leads nicely into the following track.

'Ladytron' starts with a swirling synth sound over which a mournful oboe solo can be heard while what sounds like a Mellotron (unlisted on the album cover) adds some tension before Ferry slips in with his opening vocal of 'You've got me girl on the run around' before the band slip in with some smooth backing and a run down the keyboard from Eno. It's on this track (and especially the 2018 Steven Wilson remix) that you hear Eno's manipulation of the other instruments through his VCS3. The track almost feels like it could be played in some exotic lounge club until its ending begins to pick up momentum and Manzanera's big chords thrash in and Eno's synth clunks away like a malfunctioning robot.

'If There Is Something' starts an almost country and western sound with plenty of slide guitar from Manzanera and some honky-tonk piano from Ferry. It's not until after the first instrumental break that the song changes mood totally with a wonderful sax and synth riff courtesy of Mackay and Eno. It's even here that Ferry's vocals change considerably to become more melodramatic until they reach a fever-pitched high during the song's final segment as the band almost begin to drop out to leave Thompson's beat and Ferry's vocals melodically high in its register. Here you can hear Eno's vocals clear in the 'when we were young' segment as the song comes to its end with a swelling Mellotron. '2.H.B.' enters with an electric piano riff that sounds fairly melancholic, until Ferry starts to sing about Humphrey Bogart, the 'HB' of the song's title. The song moves at a languid pace compared to the rest of the album so far and this song even sounds like the catchiest thing the band had done so far. An ambling middle section of piano and sax with subtle electronics by Eno drifts along in an almost ambient way. The song slowly fades out on an echoed piano and gives a nice gentle ending to the first side of the album.

Side two of the album feels like a slightly different beast altogether. 'The Bob (Medley)' starts off with major barre chords to which Ferry adds a rather strained angst-ridden vocal. This dilutes into an experimental section with Mackay's oboe and sax wandering over violent white noise and electronics by Eno. It feels more avant-garde than anything heard on the first side, and the next part is a jaunty rocker that wouldn't have been out of place on a Pink Fairies album. This moves into a slight piano étude that leads back to the opening section. It certainly sounds like four pieces randomly thrown together even though it's only credited to Ferry and it feels more like a band composition from parts of jamming sessions pulled together. 'Chance Meeting' is a melancholic song with Ferry's piano and vocal at the fore and has a slight Berlin cabaret vibe about it. Manzanera's guitar is treated by Eno's VCS3 and sounds spectral, hovering above Ferry's mournful piano.

'Would You Believe?' is more of a straight-ahead rocker with Ferry's vocals in its high register and with Mackay's sax and Thompson's drums dominating the breaks, again, we can clearly hear Eno doing doo-wop style backing vocals. 'Sea Breezes' starts with Eno's tape of his VCS3 making white noise wave sounds over which Ferry plays a sad electric piano and Mackay adds a delicate oboe. It's certainly one of Roxy's most beautiful early songs that sends shivers down the spine. The space in the sound and the atmosphere all feel very Eno-like and it's often been said that this is the track in which he had most influence over the recording. Thompson's odd drum pattern hits in and takes the song into a slightly more atonal territory as Eno's synth makes industrial noises beneath Manzanera's jagged guitar. Eno's vocals appear prominently on 'Bitters End', a slight piano song where again Mackay's sax dominates, and with its slight flamenco touch, it's an interesting way to finish an album that plays around with different styles.

This is certainly the most repackaged album by Roxy Music over the years, with a super-deluxe version featuring demos, out-takes, sessions and a BBC In Concert session from August of 1972, as well as a DVD and a 132-page book. At one point, the non-album single 'Virginia Plain' was added on to the track listing between 'If There Is Something' and '2.H.B.'; this is the case with the rare Steven Wilson mix of the album that brings Eno's synth and Manzanera's guitar more to the fore sound-wise and is now being treated as the 'go to' version by Eno fans.

Before the album was released, Roxy began to start gigging regularly, kicking off with an explosive performance at the Lincoln Festival on 27 May that gave them some rave reviews. They also started supporting David Bowie on some of the dates of his Ziggy Stardust tour, playing venues like

The Croydon Greyhound in what must have been some of the most glam rock concerts ever performed.

When the album was finally released on 16 June, Roxy were a quarter of the way into a two-month concert schedule that also saw them perform on the BBC's *The Old Grey Whistle Test* TV show on the 20th introduced by the underwhelmed presenter 'whispering' Bob Harris. 16 June also saw the release of David Bowie's *The Rise And Fall Of Ziggy Stardust And The Spiders From Mars*, which must make this date the year zero for all glam rock fans.

Eno discussed the reaction to the band live with Steve Peacock of *Sounds* music paper on 1 July 1972:

But there seems to be a kind of mass decision with an audience where they decide as soon as you come on stage whether they're going to be cool or enthuse – it really doesn't seem like that sometimes. We've had nights where we've played well and not been particularly well-received, and then other times we've made many mistakes, instruments have been missing from three numbers in a row, and they've really dug it. But then, Roxy aren't the easiest band to get to grips with, especially in a support band set.

On 29 July in *Melody Maker*, Eno set out his stall for his future career to Richard Williams when describing his role within the band:

At the moment, I'm mostly interested in modifying the sound of other instruments. You get a nice quality – the skill of the performer, transformed by the electronics. Neither the player nor I know what the other is going to do – which means you get some nice accidents.

On 4 August, Island released two tracks as a 7" single, but neither appeared on the album and one is a song not credited to Ferry.

'Virginia Plain' (Ferry) b/w *'The Numberer'* (Mackay)
Recorded: 10–12 July 1972
Produced by Peter Sinfield
Highest Chart Position: UK: 4

'Virginia Plain' is the song that catapulted Roxy to the big time and gave them their first *Top of the Pops* appearance later that month and got them to number four in the UK charts on 19th August. It is a rabble-rousing call to arms that diluted the entire Roxy sound into under three minutes of perfect glam pop. Ferry's bashed-out piano, Thompson's steady beat, Manzanera's rock 'n' roll guitar, Mackay's wailing sax and oboe and Eno's synth flourishes that reaches its apotheosis in its five-note riff near the end – it was Roxy perfection. The song title was based upon a painting that Ferry had done which he gave a 'slightly imponderable lyric' too. The song does reference one of Warhol's superstars, Baby Jane Holzer, who is mentioned a couple of times. The song was also the first to feature new bass player Rik Kenton after the departure of Simpson in early March.

'The Numberer' is an avant rocker that uses Eno's synth prominently throughout and utilises every band member in a slight solo spot, including Ferry on harmonica. It's an interesting instrumental piece that certainly shows the dynamic of the band at that point, all pulling together as equals as they strived to hit the big time.

The album hit its highest point of number ten in the UK charts, which was probably boosted by the single doing well and the fact that the band supported Bowie at his ambitious Rainbow shows in London on 19 and 20 of August before they headed out on their own headlining tour in October and November. The band had also started picking up press coverage in the USA, but the album was not released until later in the year there, with 'Virginia Plain' added to it and Kenton's photo replacing Simpson's on the inside of the gatefold sleeve. In December, the band headed for their first US tour, which saw them playing dates until 3 January 1973. It was on this tour that the cracks began to grow between Eno and Ferry's relationship, that pointed its way to a tumultuous year ahead for the band.

In August, Steve Peacock of *Sounds* music paper quizzed Eno about the first Roxy album and the future of their musical style:

SP: When I last talked to you, you were saying that from the starting point of the album, the music could go two ways – either the 'Ladytron' idea or the 'Re-Make/Re-Model' way. Do you think the band has developed in either direction, or are both things still fairly equal?
Eno: It's doing both, actually, and 'If There Is Something' has become a strange creature too; it's modified into something else completely, which isn't either of those two, and isn't a cross between the two either. It's Grand Music if you know what I mean; it's got a feeling of grandness about it which is hinted on the album but which has developed even

more now. I don't think, in fact, that what we do is going to get any more specific; in fact, I hope it's going to get less specific. The only style I'd like to have is one that deals with other styles, if you see what I mean – I'd like it to be said that our style is to be able to work with every style and to work with them, integrate them into our way of playing.

For Your Pleasure and (No Pussyfooting) 1973

To say that Roxy's first US tour didn't go as well as they might have hoped was an understatement. The band were booked on the support slot on some dates with the more denim-friendly audience of Edgar Winter, Jo Jo Gunne and English rockers Humble Pie and Jethro Tull. The US bookers didn't really have an idea of how to place British glam artists and Roxy's American label equated glam rock with Alice Cooper. The band even had to put up with having a fire-eater onstage with them at a gig at the Whisky a Go Go. Despite some good reviews for the album, Roxy landed in the States as an almost unknown quantity, although Eno had already started to do press there, praising the place as quoted in Dave Sheppard's book:

> I feel that there are two places I'm emotionally based in, and one is the English countryside where I was born and bred, and the other is the heart of New York City …

By the end of the 1970s, Eno relocated to New York. The tour was a hard slog to try and break Roxy there, and the only person who seemed to do well from it was Eno. He gave interviews to several music papers and seemed to indulge in quite a lot of hedonistic activity, apart from a couple of incidents down South where Eno's look didn't go down well.

Eno seemed to have a slightly more successful tour. It was Eno who became the centre of attention when Warner's did manage to get the band any press, and this was beginning to annoy Ferry as, after all, he had started the band and had written all the songs. Ferry says in Sheppard's book:

> I never liked the interview process, whereas Brian was really making a meal of it. He loved to talk and people loved to talk to him because he's very engaging. Of course, that was actually a great asset to the band, but it didn't seem like it to me at the time.

On the band's return from the States, Eno started to give interviews about what happened there (and about a woman called Cassandra who had followed him to the UK) and about the various new ideas and projects that he had a careful record of in his notebooks. Most of these ideas were already extracurricular activities beyond Roxy. In an interview with the *NME*'s Nick Kent that was published on 3 February, Eno also discussed his love for 'discipline and bondage', which helped create the persona of him being an extravagant, intellectual sex beast. Some of this imagery would be in evidence on Eno's first two post-Roxy releases.

By the middle of February, Roxy were back in the studio to record their follow-up album and this time, EG decided to money in Roxy by booking them into George Martin's AIR Studios on Oxford Street, London. The producer this time was Chris Thomas, fresh from mixing Pink Floyd's *Dark Side Of The Moon* and John Anthony, who had produced Genesis' first three albums. By the time the band entered the studio, the album already had the working title of *For Your Pleasure*. Apart from the title track and the song 'In Every Dream Home A Heartache', most of the album was put together in the studio and with more time and money to experiment, the band could create a larger sonic canvas.

But halfway through the sessions, EG and Island decided to rush release two tracks that would not find their way onto the album and give Roxy their second *Top of the Pops* performance.

'Pyjamarama' (Ferry) b/w 'The Pride And The Pain' (Mackay)

Produced by Chris Thomas and John Anthony (although only Anthony is mentioned on the disc)
Released on 23 February 1973
Highest Chart Position: UK: 10

Eno has always stated that he thought that this single sounded poor because he felt it was rush-released so that Island could capitalise on the band's UK success. He says that initial mixes and band run-throughs sound better than this standalone 7". It was the first song that Ferry had written on guitar rather than his usual piano. The song starts with some fine crash chords and drumming by Thompson, but it's the sound of Roxy scuttling towards a slightly smoother sound than on the album that follows. Only Mackay's sax solo fed through Eno's VCS3 seems to hint at any experimentation and certainly doesn't have the flair or the synthesizer stabs of 'Virginia Plain'. 'The Pride And The Pain' is a moody Mackay piece based on the score for the film *El Cid* that shows off a melancholic oboe and piano over Eno's chirping electronics. Manzanera's guitar is soulful and Ferry and Eno sing in harmony on what feels like a heavenly choir. It's another wonderful Mackay instrumental and something that has a similar atmosphere to instrumental pieces recorded by UK band Japan six years later.

As the album began recording, Rik Kenton had just left the band after returning from the US in January, so Ferry had to pull in an old friend of his, John Porter, to play bass on the album. He was listed as a guest artist and his photo did not appear on the album sleeve. In mid-March, Roxy began a 22-date tour of the UK, taking in the nation's city halls. They were on the crest of a wave not only with the fans but also with the British music press as well. On 23 March, Island Records released *For Your Pleasure* while the band were in the middle of their tour. It was the last Roxy album to feature Eno.

Roxy Music: For Your Pleasure (1973)

Personnel:
Bryan Ferry: voice, keyboards
Andrew Mackay: oboe, saxophone
Eno: synthesizer, tapes
Paul Thompson: drums
Phil Manzanera: guitar
Guest artiste – John Porter: bass
Produced by: Chris Thomas
Recorded at: AIR Studios, London, February 1973
Released: 23 March 1973
Highest Chart Position: UK: 4; USA: 193
Tracklisting. Side One: 1. Do The Strand; 2. Beauty Queen; 3. Strictly Confidential; 4. Editions Of You; 5. In Every Dream Home A Heartache. Side Two: 1. The Bogus Man; 2. Grey Lagoons; 3. For Your Pleasure
Words and music by Bryan Ferry

The second Roxy Music album opens with the bluster and stomp of one of their finest songs, 'Do The Strand'. With Ferry at his suave best as he sings about a made-up dance in the tradition of an artist from the fifties. The song references the *Mona Lisa*, the book *Lolita* and Picasso's painting of *Guernica,* as well as other famous dance routines. The song is the band in full charge ahead mode with Eno's synth playing subtly running throughout and some wonderful guitar work, treated by Eno, from Manzanera. It was released as a single in America and a lot later here in the UK.

'Beauty Queen' is one of Roxy's laid-back ethereal numbers that self-references 'Sea Breezes' from the first album, including Eno making his VCS3 wave sound again. This is Ferry at his most lounge lizard sounding vocally, his piano playing is exquisite and the song points ahead to the Roxy sound after Eno departed.

'Strictly Confidential' is one of those Ferry songs that hangs in the air, creating an atmosphere of its own. Eno can be heard on the backing vocals and adding atmospheric touches on the synth and tapes. This is the band in a slightly maudlin vibe, but Manzanera's guitar and Mackay's oboe lift the track from any sombre feeling. 'Editions Of You' is the band's tour de force and features some great Ferry vocals, again backed by Eno. There are some wonderful solo slots from Mackay on sax and Manzanera on guitar, but it's Eno's ear-piercing synth wailing that steals the show and sends shivers down the spine.

'In Every Dream Home A Heartache' is Ferry's paean to an inflatable sex doll but can also be viewed as a critique of the emptiness of opulence and the loneliness of modern living. Its moody D# F#F#G# chord progression that is cyclical adds a brooding atmosphere to Ferry's almost monotone delivered lyrics. The song shifts gear when Ferry sings, 'I blew up your body, But you blew my mind' and is taken over by an extended solo. The song was performed on *The Old Grey Whistle Test* and is probably the song by Roxy that has been most covered by other bands.

Side two starts with 'The Bogus Man', the most experimental track on the album, and the one that feels like it has Eno's influence written all over it. Eno and Mackay wanted to carry on doing more experimental pieces, but Ferry was trying to streamline the band's sound with one eye on the more commercial market; this was another area where Eno and Ferry butted heads at this point. Ferry's vocals are in their high pitch register and the music almost has that Weimar sound again, with Eno's synth punching in the bottom end and Mackay's atonal sax playing. It was good that Roxy were still pushing boundaries, but this would grow less with each subsequent album as the band became more polished.

'Grey Lagoons' features Eno prominently on backing vocals, again doing lots of 'aaahhhs' to what is a more formulaic Roxy song from this era, and one you can almost sense was put together in the studio rather than a composition written earlier by Ferry. A harmonica and synth duel breaks out at one point, but this is more of a standard rocker than anything else on the album. Eno is very present on the album's closing track 'For Your Pleasure' with his synths and treatments and the most obvious use of echo and delay that became an Eno production forte during the seventies. The song ends with the taped voice of actress Judi Dench saying, 'You don't ask. You don't ask why.' Again, Eno's backing vocals are prominent and the song could almost be a track on his first solo album for the kind of style it evokes; his synth sound also closes the album.

For many, *For Your Pleasure* is Roxy's masterwork. Even Ferry has said that it is his favourite Roxy album. Ferry also complimented Eno's performance on the album, as quoted in Sheppard's book:

Brian's stuff on that one was especially great. His keyboards on 'Do The Strand', all his stuff on the 'Bogus Man' – really, really great.

The cover was also one of Roxy's most striking, Ferry's then-girlfriend Amanda Lear striding in high heels and black leather with a panther in front of her towards a waiting limo which has Ferry dressed as a chauffeur, reeked of the kind of style that Roxy was becoming famous for. Its inner gatefold showed the band in all their glam glory, each holding a guitar (except for Mackay). Eno looks the most androgenous, his wonderful make-up and peacock-feathered jacket standing out, as does his waif-like thin torso; he was the man closest to Bowie at this point for glam outrageousness, and he oozes sensuality as he gazes straight at the camera.

By the time the band's tour reached the Rainbow Theatre in London, Roxy mania had begun to hit Britain. This time the band even had a set designed for them full of diaphanous drapes that, during the set go-go dancers would appear from; even Amanda Lear clad in a G-string and high heels, introduced the band onstage by announcing 'Ladies and Gentlemen, for your pleasure … Roxy Music'. It was the apotheosis of Roxy mania with Eno in the band, but storm clouds were already beginning to gather around them.

In the spring of 1973, the band headed off for a European tour starting in Italy. Rather than the slog of the US tour, Roxy were already ascending stars in Europe, so they stayed in the finest hotels and ate in the best restaurants; this was Roxy as glamorous idols, even meeting surrealist artist Salvador Dali along the way. It is also on this tour that Eno would be seen with a different woman every day, much to Ferry's annoyance. Ferry began to leave after-show parties early, while Eno would stay to entertain. The two men were now barely speaking to each other as the tour rolled on, even though the tour was a massive success; the press, though sometimes referred to Roxy as 'Eno's band', and this must have further irked Ferry. The tour concluded in Amsterdam on 26 May and this was one of the last of Eno's shows with the band. He was already aware that his days as a Roxy musician may be numbered because of his crumbling relationship with Ferry. Back in the UK, the band played at the York festival in June. Little did anyone know that Ferry had asked teenage keyboard prodigy Eddie Jobson to observe Eno's playing from the side of the stage. The show was a disaster for Ferry as the audience started to chant Eno's name during the quieter songs and Ferry got angrier. Eno tried to get the audience to calm down but to no avail. After the encores, Ferry stormed off into the wings swearing; Ferry's attitude after the show was to freeze Eno out of the band.

With Ferry on a long holiday in Corfu, Eno realised that the situation between the two of them had become unworkable. On 23 July 1973, Eno called a meeting with the band's management EG and, after talks, informed them that he would be leaving the band. Years later, Ferry discusses Eno's departure in Sheppard's book:

> Looking back, it was a shame that EG didn't get me and Brian together and say, 'Look, on the positive side, you've got this, on the negative side, you've got that ... you can do a solo album with Eddie Jobson ... maybe there's a way of keeping the band together as it is.' They never got us together to discuss it at all.

In truth, most critics and band members felt they had at least another two albums with Eno as a member, but it wasn't to be and from here on Roxy would take a different voyage, slowly moving their sound away from the first two albums that had made them so huge in the UK and Europe. Eno has said that the whole band had a unique chemistry together, but in some sense, Eno was relieved to leave the Roxy treadmill as he could now put into action all the ideas he had been making notes about for the last two years. As soon as he got home from the EG meeting, he began a cathartic bout of songwriting. In his first endeavour, he created the song 'Baby's On Fire'. With this creation, Eno was now a fully-fledged solo artist.

However, before Eno could immerse himself in the recording of his first solo album, he had some unfinished business with King Crimson leader and guitarist Robert Fripp to attend to first. The pair had met in 1972 and Eno had invited the progressive rock legend to his home studio on 8 September. Fripp had brought along his guitar and added it to some tape delay looping tracks he had prepared in the mode of Terry Riley and Pauline Oliveros. Eno selectively looped Fripp's guitar to give the effect of multi-layered recordings; it was a procedure that Eno christened 'Frippertronics'. Together they created a 21-minute piece that they would call 'The Heavenly Music Corporation'. It was a dense, almost ambient piece.

By August 1973, Fripp was growing bored with Crimson and the endless touring, and finding himself back in London, he contacted Eno, who he knew was now free from Roxy, to continue their experimentation together. This time, the pair went to Command Studios on 4 and 5 August to work on another 20-minute track of ambient music, this time with Fripp playing along to an electronic background loop of Eno's VCS3. For Eno, this was the perfect way to get a cheap record released and keep his name out there in the public eye, post-Roxy, in the ever-fickle rock 'n' roll market.

After this initial recording, the pair made their way to AIR Studios to mix the track they had recorded, David Sheppard explains one of the titles:

En route, Eno had picked up a discarded page ripped from a fetish magazine that was lying in the Oxford Street gutter. It bore the phrase 'Swastika Girls' and on the reverse was a photo of a girl in bondage wearing a Nazi armband giving a 'Sieg Heil' salute – an image which chimed with Eno's current predilection for all things provocatively sadomasochistic. The picture was placed on the mixing desk throughout the session and 'Swastika Girls' was duly adopted as the title for the new piece.

Fripp & Eno: (No Pussyfooting) (1973)

Personnel:
Robert Fripp: guitar
Brian Eno: tapes, VCS3
Produced by: Fripp & Eno
Recorded at: Eno's Studio 8 September 1972 and Command Studios 4 and 5 September 1973
Released: November 1973
Highest Chart Position: –
Tracklisting: Side One: 1. The Heavenly Music Corporation. Side Two: 1. Swastika Girls

The album's title comes from a note that Fripp had stuck on his guitar pedalboard during the recording sessions. The cover was another deluxe gatefold release for Island with a photo of the duo in what was called the infinite room, playing cards with a set of pornographic playing cards, one of which would find its way onto Eno's first solo album. The photo taken by Willie Christie shows Eno still wearing his trademark Roxy make-up, with the duo being shot in three different poses – the back cover shot is of the room minus the musicians.

'The Heavenly Music Corporation' features Fripp on guitar only, with Eno manipulating his sound via tape loops. The piece bases itself around a drone over which Fripp's fretboard work manoeuvres in a fairly languid fashion as it dances around the air and creates a majestic atmosphere.

'Swastika Girls' has a more prominent Eno input into the track as it begins with his VCS3 giving electronic bleeps as it loops around. Steadily, Fripp's guitar begins to build over the electronic wash of sound beneath it. The track feels like it has more going on than the first side, with the guitar chimes looping over the backing synth. Here Fripp's playing seems to use more distortion than on the previous track and his playing seems a little more rock.

Before its release, John Peel was given a tape of the album to play the whole of it on his show, but by mistake, the tape was actually played backwards, meaning that Peel's listeners heard 40 minutes of Fripp & Eno in reverse. Later a version of this would turn up on a limited CD release of the album.

When the tapes of the album were handed to Island Records, they were less than happy with it, especially as it would end up being released only a couple of months before Eno's first 'proper' solo album with songs on. Island thought this might confuse potential buyers of his first album. In the end, they released the album at a discounted price and it was promoted more like a novelty record rather than a serious work of art, but the record would still sell 100,000 copies though. The reviews for the album were mixed with some wondering what it was all about. When it was released, even at a discounted price, the album failed to chart in the UK, meaning that Island began to hold their collective breath for Eno's own solo release.

Over the years, the album has grown in stature and is seen as one of the first ambient rock albums. It has also been dissected by many writers of experimental music, with 'The Heavenly Music Corporation' being hailed as the better work. Eric Tamm in his 1995 book *Brian Eno, His Music and the Vertical Colour of Sound*, has this to say about 'Swastika Girls':

It is less successful than the earlier piece, it is because of the much greater overall saturation of the acoustic space. There seems to be a perceptual rule that possibilities for appreciation of timbral subtleties decrease in proportion to the rate of actual notes being played. 'Swastika Girls' shows Eno and Fripp had not yet understood the full weight of this principle.

But for Eno, the reviews mattered little while he was ensconced in Majestic Studios in London recording and then planning the release of his first album *Here Come The Warm Jets*, an album that had only taken him 12 days to record and would be one of his biggest-selling releases.

It is here we run into a slight problem about when the album was released, as some references say it was released in November 1973 while others say the beginning of 1974, with one site claiming that it was released in January.

It seems that the album had a delayed release due to the OPEC oil embargo that had delayed quite a few albums from their official release date, some even having them pushed back twice. Also, *Melody Maker* at the time doesn't list the album as available in late 1973. Eno and Russell Mills' 1986 book *More Dark Than Shark* has the release date as 1973, although it appears to have charted in the UK on 9 March 1974, meaning a release closer to this time. So, I'm going to hedge my bets and place the album release as 1974 and discuss it in the next chapter.

Chapter 4: Here Come The Warm Jets and Taking Tiger Mountain (By Strategy) 1974

As it turned out, 1974 was a hectic and tumultuous year for Eno and one where he expanded his sound. He undertook a disastrous tour and began to reinvent himself in the process as he slowly began to slip away from the glam rocker of the past couple of years. He would have a documentary about him appear in cinemas showing his working methods during the making of his first solo album in September 1973.

First and foremost was the delayed release of *Here Come The Warm Jets*, an album that featured 16 musicians in total and proved to any doubters that Eno could knock out a good tune as well as be Mr Glam Avant-Garde. Among those musicians used were his ex-Roxy bandmates, Simon King of Hawkwind, Bill MacCormick from Canterbury progressive rock band Matching Mole, Paul Rudolph from The Pink Fairies, Fripp and John

Wetton from King *Crimson and members of the rock band Sharks.* In a *Melody Maker* interview with Geoff Brown on 10 November 1973, Eno discussed the creation of his first solo album and what he learned from venturing out on his own in the studio:

> I learnt very much doing this album. I did it very quickly. I recorded it in twelve days, so it's quite a cheap album. Empirically, I know what sounds I want, though in technical terms, I might not be able to express them as well.

Eno: Here Come The Warm Jets (1974)

Personnel:
Brian Eno: vocals, keyboards, guitar (snake), electric larynx, synthesizer, treatments
Phil Manzanera: guitar
Chris 'Ace' Spedding: guitar
Robert Fripp: guitar
Bill MacCormick: bass
Simon King: percussion
Busta Cherry Jones: bass
Marty Simon: percussion
John Wetton: bass
Paul Rudolph: bass
Nick Judd: keyboards
Andy Mackay: saxophone, keyboards
Paul Thompson: percussion
Lloyd Watson: slide guitar
Chris Thomas: bass
Sweetfeed: backing vocals
All songs written by Brian Eno unless stated
Produced by: Brian Eno
Recorded at: Majestic Studios, London
Released: February 1974
Highest Chart Position: UK: 26; USA: 151
Tracklisting: Side One: 1. Needles In The Camel's Eye (Eno, Manzanera); 2. The Paw Paw Negro Blowtorch; 3. Baby's On Fire; 4. Cindy Tells Me (Eno, Manzanera); 5. Driving Me Backwards. Side Two: 1. On Some Faraway Beach; 2. Blank Frank (Eno, Fripp); 3. Dead Finks Don't Talk; 4. Some Of Them Are Old; 5. Here Come The Warm Jets

The meaning of the title of the album is most often thought of as a reference to the cover art, which features a 'naughty' playing card with a photo of a woman urinating outside. This card sits in front of a black-and-white photo of Eno still in very much his glam peacock phase, surrounded by various surreal items; in the background, you can see Eno's heavily made-up face reflected in a mirror.

The album begins with the aural assault that is 'Needles In The Camel's Eye' with his heavy guitar battering ram of sound. Eno explains its lyrics in his book *More Dark Than Shark*:

> What can I tell you about this inexplicable lyric? It was written in less time than it takes to sing. The word 'needles' was picked up from the guitar sound, which to me is reminiscent of a cloud of metal needles. Phil Manzanera played and I beat his tremolo-arm rhythmically with my hand.

'The Paw Paw Negro Blowtorch' is based upon a story that Eno had read about a man who had an ailment where his breath caused things to ignite. Musically it is closer to the first Roxy Music album with big barre chords and a wonderful atonal VCS3 solo from Eno. A chirping synth sound segues the previous track into the album's tour de force 'Baby's On Fire', the song where Fripp's fret work is allowed to explode in what some people claim is his greatest lead guitar break. According to Eno, the song is about a book he was reading on spontaneous combustion. The overall sound of the track is one of urgency, with the two drums playing against each other and the Morse code-like figure of Eno's synth.

'Cindy Tells Me', is in the vein of an old fifties song, with its slightly doo-wop and Shangri-Las type of feel. The lyrics discuss an empty existence that is only uplifted by the buying of time-saving gadgets. This is a critique of the bored, wealthy housewife syndrome that was becoming more apparent in agony columns and was being satirised in family sitcoms of the time. 'Driving Me Backwards' is based around some heavily treated piano chords, almost sounding like an old pub upright that you would find in public houses during the wartime period. Eno explains the lyrics in 1986's *More Dark Than Shark*:

> A mixture of a series of thoughts about controlled existence – the desirability of being stripped of choice if you like. 'Chemical choices' indicates choice without volition. It is based on another song I wrote (but didn't record) played backwards.

'On Some Faraway Beach' is the most obviously romantic and melancholic song on the album, with its piano taking the main theme and Eno's mournful opening lyric 'Given the chance, I'll die like a baby, On some far away beach'. The song is quite moving with a great vocal from Eno and the slow pointing towards the direction his music would slowly begin to take. 'Blank Frank' is Eno back at his abrasive best with a lyric about a small-time Ipswich gangster who was hired to beat up people for relatively small amounts of money. The track was recorded in reverse to the normal way where instruments are recorded in the studio, which usually means laying down a rhythm section first. Instead, it was Fripp's guitar work and Eno's vocals that were put down first and the closing organ section was played by four non-keyboard players, all hitting notes at the same time.

'Dead Finks Don't Talk' is probably more famous today because of Eno doing an impersonation of his old band leader, Ferry during one of the lines of the lyrics. The track is also the only one on the album to feature Eno's old bandmate Paul Thompson on drums (who also gets an arrangement credit). The lyrics are about 'being ambitious and smarmy at the same time' according to Eno, so one wonders if the Ferry vocal was deliberately used for this particular lyric. 'Some Of Them Are Old' has lots of hanging chord sequences played by Mackay, who also supplies some wonderful saxophone, and it's another downward feeling song with lyrics that seem to discuss fame, loss and regret all at the same time. It's where people visit and take a little of your soul when they depart. The song shifts into 'Here Come The Warm Jets', an instrumental that gives a signpost to Eno's next direction. With guitar and bass played by ex-Pink Fairies guitarist Paul Rudolph, the track has a feel of wide-open spaces, and a certain feel of ambience about it, and a touching way to finish the album.

Critical reception for the album was mostly positive and the album crept up the charts reaching its peak position on 9 March. Eno had managed to blend avant-garde experimentalism with foot-stomping glam rock with ease, but it was now felt that he should go out on the road and promote the album. In January, Eno visited a pub and watched a band called The Winkies play and he was impressed with their musicianship enough to approach them about being his backing band for a few dates beginning in February to promote the delayed album. After the band agreed, Eno rushed them to the studio to work on a 7" single that would be released in March to coincide with the tour and also to be his backing band for an up-and-coming John Peel session. The single would eventually be released on 22 March, but by that point, the tour finished prematurely.

'Seven Deadly Finns' (Eno) b/w 'Later On' (Eno)

Release date: 22 March 1974
Produced by: Eno
Highest Chart Position: –

Eno's first solo single almost touches the Top 40 and is a wonderful three minutes of glam sleaze proto-punk backed by The Winkies. The song itself has many references to sexual acts and uses American 'hooker slang' to describe them and is probably the only single ever to reach the Top 100 using the word 'systemically'. The backing vocals are provided by Eno's friend Judy Nylon who would also appear on a couple of his other releases. The narrative is about seven Finnish sailors who visit a French bordello, and the song would also reference Japanese pornography, something that Eno had become particularly keen on. The song is a joyous barrage of rock with some fine yodelling from Eno at the end of the track. 'Later On' was culled from the Fripp & Eno sessions and was a tape collage Eno had prepared at home and then added some vocal undulations on to give the track an extra element that the album never had. Eno would be seen later in the year performing 'Seven Deadly Finns' on Dutch television; this has now become a kind of unofficial promo video for the song and Eno can be seen miming wearing a fairly flamboyant Japanese-style outfit, a beret and quite a bit of make-up.

On 26 February 1974, Eno and The Winkies headed into the studio to record three tracks for a John Peel session – these included 'The Paw Paw Negro Blowtorch', 'Baby's On Fire/Totalled' and a cover version of the Peggy Lee song 'Fever', it was broadcast on 5 March and has been widely bootlegged over the years with Eno's other radio sessions.

At the end of February, Eno and The Winkies started their brief and ill-fated tour of the UK. Eno would be centre stage next to his beloved VCS3 and AKS synthesizer set-up. Eno looked immaculate each night dressed in a variety of outfits and many in the audience were surprised just how good his vocals were in a live setting. Unfortunately, not many people got to see him perform as the tour only lasted five dates. After a concert at the Croydon Greyhound, Eno was overcome by excruciating chest pains, so he was taken to university hospital and was told one of his lungs had collapsed. The remainder of the tour and the continental dates that had also been added were all cancelled while Eno lay in hospital with tubes draining fluid from his chest cavity. To recuperate, Eno packed himself off on a holiday and began to reconsider his career path and what he wanted to do next. From here on in, Eno became a studio-based recording artist with only a handful of live dates that he played throughout the rest of the seventies.

On Eno's return to the UK, he had a meeting with Island Records and discovered that they had recently signed Nico and John Cale, ex-members of Eno's favourite band, The Velvet Underground, and soon Eno performed live at a one-off event with his heroes. A&R man Richard Williams saw the potential in getting the three together and also helping out a financially strapped ex-Soft Machine member Kevin Ayers at the same time. The idea was to record a live album showing off the label's new signings and keep Eno's name in the public profile as well as helping to try and recoup some of Ayers's lost money, so a gig was hastily organised for 1 June 1974, at the Rainbow Theatre, London, so a recording could be made. The press dubbed the evening ACNE after using the names of the band members. Sheppard describes the atmosphere at rehearsals:

> Eno would later deem the project conceptually under-prepared, hinting that, although the rehearsal had been thorough, drugs and inflamed egos had made their mark.

It seems that tensions between Cale and Ayers came to a head during the rehearsals, with Ayers seducing his wife, which makes his sonic howl performance of 'Heartbreak Hotel' (with Eno on the trusty VCS3) more poignant. At the concert itself, Eno was still resplendent in his glam glad rags and make-up and was warmly welcomed onstage as he performed 'Driving Me Backwards', with Cale on viola, and a barnstorming version of 'Baby's On Fire'. Eno also played on Nico's haunting rendition of The Doors' song 'The End'. The live album, which was released just before Christmas, featured all of these songs (these were a lot less than most of the sets played) and a whole side of Kevin Ayers's folk rock featuring Mike Oldfield on guitar. The album sadly failed to chart and is now seen a curio in the collection of all four artists. For Eno, it was another stopgap before he could start working on his next proper album but at least he got to play onstage with a couple of his heroes. Later that summer, Eno appeared on Cale's first solo album *Fear*, which was produced by Phil Manzanera, and Nico's album *Desertshore* produced by Cale. Some European live dates followed with the pair, including an incredible avant-garde performance in Berlin, and in only two years, Eno was back there for a very different reason.

Also around this time were the first cinema screenings of a 30-minute documentary simply called *Eno* directed by Alfons Sinniger. The film focuses on the making of *Here Come The Warm Jets* the previous year, and shows Eno in the studio, putting his make-up on at home, fiddling with his VCS3, shopping in Portobello Market, and preparing for a concert with the Portsmouth Sinfonia. The documentary has appeared on YouTube a couple of times but for some reason tends to get removed after only a few weeks. It is an excellent window into Eno's life post-Roxy Music with some great sound bites from the man and a rare look into how he was making albums at the time.

Eno's next phase was to concentrate on his second solo album, but this time he would use fewer guest musicians as his songwriting became stronger. One of his new recruits was Genesis drummer Phil Collins, who was asked to join the recording sessions after Eno had a cast a little magic over the band's *The Lamb Lies Down On Broadway* album after he was asked to join the sessions by singer Peter Gabriel. For this album, Eno also began to use the 'first person' style of lyric writing, which gave the record a more personal feel even if most of the lyrics were still fairly esoteric. The title of the album was taken from a postcard of a Chinese Maoist opera called *Taking Tiger Mountain By Strategy*, yet another piece of Eno happenstance. The more Eno considered the title, the more he felt he could base a rough conceptual work around it, using the idea as a working base for the songs that would make up the album. Manzanera was called back on board to help produce and to add his guitar flourishes as well, even Mackay was back to add some brass to one of the tracks.

Taking Tiger Mountain (By Strategy) was recorded during September 1974, it was also the first Eno album that utilised the 'Oblique Strategies' cards that he had designed with artist Peter Schmidt. These were a series of statements that were written on a set of cards and were shuffled and drawn to maybe help blockages in the recording process or to throw up new ideas if Eno felt the track was getting a bit stale. With cards reading such things as 'honour thy error as a hidden intention' and 'work at a different speed', these were utilised in the studio to take a particular piece of music in a different direction. Schmidt himself went on to design the cover for *Taking Tiger Mountain...* making it an iconic gatefold sleeve design for Eno.

Sheppard discusses Eno's process during the writing of the album:

As soon as he'd outlined its musical shape, Eno would take a piece of paper and make a plan – a flow chart – of the song, sketching the places where lyrics would sit best. Then, with trusty Dictaphone in hand, he would play back the song and – when he reached the allotted parts – sing whatever came into his head.

Eno: *Taking Tiger Mountain (By Strategy)* (1974)

Personnel:
Eno: vocals, electronics, snake guitar, keyboards, treatments
Phil Manzanera: guitar
Brian Turrington: bass
Freddie Smith: drums
Robert Wyatt: percussion, backing vocals
Andy Mackay: brass on track 3
Phil Collins: drums on track 4
Polly Eltes: vocals on track 4
Portsmouth Sinfonia: strings on track 7
All songs written by Brian Eno unless stated
Produced by: Brian Eno and Phil Manzanera
Recorded at: Island Studios, London
Released: November 1974
Highest Chart Position: –
Tracklisting: Side One: 1. Burning Airlines Give You So Much More, 2. Back In Judy's Jungle, 3. The Fat Lady Of Limbourg, 4. Mother Whale Eyeless, 5. The Great Pretender, Side Two: 1. Third Uncle, 2. Put A Straw Under Baby, 3. The True Wheel (Eno, Manzanera), 4. China My China, 5. Taking Tiger Mountain

There could hardly have been a more different opening track to the bombast of his first album than 'Burning Airlines Give You So Much More'. The track has a more laid-back feel about it and even Eno's synth realises the possibility of a tuneful riff at the opening and repeating throughout. According to Russell Mills in *More Dark Than Shark*:

> This song was originally called 'Turkish Airlines' based on what was, up until then, about 1974, the worst air disaster ever known – a Turkish DC-10 exploded at Orly Airport, Paris, killing all the passengers.

It was probably wise for Eno to change the theme and instead, he weaves a tale of espionage, morning tea, Japan and couples getting married, creating an oddly comforting world view of the international jet-set in 1974 in its languid pace with some fine rhythm guitar by Manzanera.

'Back In Judy's Jungle' feels like a Second World War concert party song that's drifted into a surreal Buñuel film. Eno described the track as a dance song as well as a song about the conflicting attitudes of 'emergencies' and 'opportunities' within two different groups of soldiers fighting in the jungle.

'The Fat Lady Of Limbourg' is about a woman who is an expert in some unspecified substance, Eno discusses in *More Dark Than Shark*:

Limbourg is a town in Belgium famed for its very large asylum. The inmates outnumber the townsfolk. The Fat Lady is one of the inmates, and her past may or may not be real.

Mackay's layered sax adds extra menace to a song that is already fairly dark in its nature, and again Eno flies around a surreal collection of images that wouldn't be out of place in a Jan Švankmajer animation. 'Mother Whale Eyeless' is a song about blind patriotism that manages to also reference a few movies along the way. Again, this is a more controlled song than anything on *Warm Jets* and has one of Eno's catchiest choruses thrown in for good measure. Side one ends with 'The Great Pretender', a song about the rape of a suburban housewife by a type of crazed machine. Eno gives another reading of it, also saying that the housewife is machine-like, and the Great Pretender disturbs her ordered balance in the world. This track on the original vinyl release has a locked groove at the end of it of Eno's chirping synth sound.

Side two starts with the proto-punk thrash of 'Third Uncle', a barnstorming big three-chord punch with Eno singing a collection of arbitrary sentences with conflicting images that are meaningless statements when placed beside each other. Brian Turrington gets an arrangement credit for his brilliant bass work that holds the whole track together. 'Put A Straw Under Baby' features the Portsmouth Sinfonia mangling any sense of classical music and melody throughout the song. In an odd way, it's the most avant-garde track on the album. The song discusses the putting of a piece of straw under an altar piece image of infant Jesus as a sign of homage and the orchestra tries to reflect a more classical Italian image of this musically.

Written by both Eno and Manzanera, 'The True Wheel' is the most complex song on the album. The lyrics come from a dream Eno had in a hotel in New York where a group of girls were singing the song and chanting 'We are the 801' (eight, nought, one also spells out ENO), and the lyrics also refer to the Cabala as well. Eno talks about its chord structure in *More Dark...*:

> The first is that it is constructed in a circular fashion; the main section of the song is a three-chord sequence moving round within a four-bar pattern. This means the song is always being pushed in a peculiar fashion.

Eno tries to offer no real explanation to the lyrics, although he does reference the tree of life when he has discussed it. On the song's turning point, it sounds as if the chord sequence is suddenly played in reverse or that a reversal happens at its midway point.

'China My China' is a far more straight-ahead rock song than the preceding tracks. The lyric seems to be discussing Western ideas or knowledge of Communist China and references opium farmers and women having to type out triplicate orders, manifestos and proclamations. Its chord sequence is quite jagged and even though it was never released as a single, a promotional video was made featuring Eno singing and his friend Judy Nylon miming to the guitar lines. The album closes with 'Taking Tiger Mountain', a melancholy guitar and piano piece that ends the album on a subdued note, its lyrics talking about an imaginary ascent to the top of Tiger Mountain through the snow with Eno's vocals double-tracked to make a choir-type effect with the help of The Simplistics who are not described, so I imagine they are whoever was hanging around the studio that day.

With Schmidt's stunning gatefold of a multitude of different images of Eno (an edition of 2,000 lithograph prints were sold by Schmidt as a separate artwork) and the stripped-down musician list, this album has a very different feel than its predecessor. When it was released in November, the album appeared to sell well but apparently did not chart in the Top 50 in the UK. Eno knew this was an important album for him because he realised that his first solo outing probably sold off the back of him being an ex-Roxy member and a curious interest in what he might do. Also, this time there was no promotion tour for the album, so it would have to sell pretty much on its own merits and from the mainly positive reviews it got in the music press.

To finish the year off, Eno reunited with Fripp to begin working on their follow-up album to *(No Pussyfooting)* utilising the same way of working as the first album, although this one ended up being recorded at five different studios and felt more overly melodic than the first. The duo also began to talk about the idea of doing some live dates of purely improvisational music. This was all a very positive way to round off 1974, and then 1975 quite literally struck Eno and things would change.

Broken Head – Discreet Music, Evening Star and Another Green World 1975

1975 was a year of change for Eno, and he was involved with more projects than ever before, but he could also see the landscape changing around him. The party that was glam rock was finally coming to an end, David Bowie jettisoned his glam image and made his way via a 'plastic soul' album to his Thin White Duke phase that he would see out the seventies with. By the end of the year, he went from just being billed as 'Eno' on his albums to becoming 'Brian Eno', and even sartorially, he changed as well, as the plumage of glam gave way to a more sober look more becoming to a serious artist, although a little make-up still remained. It was also the year that Eno became more involved with studio production as well as more interested and involved in the German 'Krautrock' scene after witnessing the band Harmonia play live.

To start the year, Eno was working on Phil Manzanera's first solo album called *Diamond Head*. Eno contributed synthesizer as well as treatments and vocals on two of the album's standout tracks, 'Big Day' and 'Miss Shapiro'. However, on the evening of 18 January, after completing vocal duties on the album, Eno thought he would stroll back home to Maida Vale on a cold and icy evening. Eno was distracted, pondering the day's recording and contemplating what the year ahead might hold for him. Wearing his favourite leather-soled shoes, Eno slipped on some ice on the pavement and stumbled onto the road in front of a black cab travelling at around 40 miles per hour. The taxi struck Eno on his legs knocking him backwards where his head struck the bumper of a parked car. He lay there prone with blood pouring from his head, but luckily some people in the pub nearby were alerted to the accident and phoned for an ambulance, although some of them thought Eno might already be dead. He was taken to a nearby hospital with his hand clutching his head. Luckily none of his injuries were life-threatening and the hole in his head had to have several stitches, but it was the second time that Eno had found himself in hospital in just ten months.

A little over a week later, Eno discharged himself from hospital, going to Grantully Road to convalesce, armed with painkillers, and he would spend most of the winter flat on his back pondering his own future and mortality. This would also lead to the often-repeated story by Eno himself of how he discovered ambient music, which he describes on the sleeve notes to his album *Discreet Music*:

In January this year, I had an accident. I was not seriously hurt, but I was confined to bed in a stiff, static position. My friend Judy Nylon visited me and bought me a record of 18th-century harp music. After she had gone, and with some considerable difficulty, I put on the record. Having laid down, I realised that the amplifier was set at an extremely low level, and one channel of the stereo had failed completely. Since I hadn't the energy to get up and improve matters, the record played on almost inaudibly. This presented what was, for me, a new way of hearing music – as part of the ambience of the environment, just as the colour of the light and sound of the rain were parts of that ambience.

This was a major revelation for Eno and one that changed the entire direction of his career from here on in. Nylon, however, refutes part of the story saying that they had set up the record to play back at a low level, so there was 'no ambience by mistake'. Whatever actually happened, this was certainly an epiphany moment for Eno and gave him food for thought while he recuperated.

By the end of March, Eno was back on his feet and on a promotional press tour of the US for his *Taking Tiger Mountain*. By April, he was fully restored to health and was eager to get back to work, getting in touch with Robert Fripp so that the pair could re-establish their recordings, this time with Eno's ambient idea becoming its major focus. The pair adjourned to Basing Street Studios to put into action Eno's new ideas about environmental music, which would create the pair's most aurally shimmering album.

It was at this point that the pair decided to reactivate their idea for some improvised live performances. The performances would be of Eno providing backdrops of elements of sound he had recorded while Fripp would improvise solo over the loop with his guitar fed through and manipulated by Eno's VCS3 synth. There were no rehearsals for the shows and each of the gigs were one-off events that could last up to two hours or maybe only 30 minutes, depending upon how the duo were feeling that particular night. The gigs kicked off at the end of May 1975 and straggled on until early June.

On 9 May, Eno was experimenting with tape loops on his Revox machines so he would have a piece that Fripp could improvise over. He came up with a slight melodic piece on the VCS3 and fed it through an old echo unit and he made subtle treatments on it using a graphic equaliser but effectively let the piece transform itself slowly (Eno even took a telephone call while he was recording it). When it was finished, he played the piece to Fripp but accidentally set the tape machine to half speed, making the music an eerie billowing symphony of sound. This would not only become a major element to the duo's track 'Wind On Wind' but would also become the entire first side to Eno's solo album *Discreet Music*.

Fripp and Eno kicked off their tour with some dates, six shows in all, in Spain and France, starting on 21 May with a show in Madrid. The pair then ambled back to the UK for a show at the Assembly Rooms in Royal Tunbridge Wells and at the London Palladium in early June. Before the shows, they met backstage 30 minutes before each performance and, over a glass or two of whisky, they thrashed out rough ideas about what they might play, although keeping their eyes and ears firmly on improvisation. The first show in Madrid petered out in about ten minutes, leaving the duo sitting there as the Revox machines played into infinity while the crowd began to hurl abuse. The performance wasn't helped by the fact that all the dates had next to no stage lighting, meaning that the duo were almost performing in the dark. A recording of a Paris Olympia show on 28 May soon began to surface as a bootleg and after many years, in 2014. Opal Music would release it on three CDs called *Fripp & Eno – Live In Paris 28.05.1975*. This presented a recording of the entire show for the first time over two CDs and was backed by a third CD of Eno's loops recorded as the backing tracks for the concerts. This gives us a glimpse of the pair at their height musically for what was their only live dates with, at least this time, an appreciative audience. The UK shows had their difficulties as well, with the local *Tunbridge Wells Courier* newspaper reporting that fans walked out during Fripp & Eno's show there.

In late June, Eno began to put down preliminary ideas for what would be his third solo album and sessions were booked for Basing Street Studios. Again, Eno pulled in an eclectic bunch of musicians to bring his ideas to life, including John Cale, Phil Collins, Percy Jones (from Collins' side project Brand X), The Winkies' Brian Turrington, Fripp (of course) and Paul Rudolph. Eno, though, found the initial sessions hard going with nothing being completed on the first three days' recording and even Eno struggled to start something from an unpromising beginning. Geeta Dayal discusses in her 2009 book *Another Green World*:

Another Green World certainly seemed like an unpromising beginning at first. Even with the impressive roster Eno assembled, and his own burgeoning talents in the studio, the sessions would either reveal themselves to be encouraging seeds, ready to burst into resplendent sonic paradise – or a complete, unremitting disaster. At the start, it looked to be the latter.

Eno had even reached a point where he was going to cancel the remaining studio time and work on the album slowly at home. He later called the making of the album an 'almost unmitigated hell', telling the *NME* in 1976 that it was terrible and 'I used to come home and cry' he said. Eno, though would yet again use his trusty Oblique Strategies to try and help him out of any musical cul-de-sacs or production problems, even though many of the pieces relied on a certain degree of improvisation.

After the initial inertia, the sessions slowly started taking a different turn and his rough sketches of ideas began to bear fruit. Eno decided that because the album was largely improvised that it was wise to abandon any pieces that he felt were not working, to hopefully pursue a new fertile path elsewhere. The more Eno began to use the studio as an instrument, the more he felt he could stretch both himself and his musicians sonically and hopefully explore avenues that they had not thought of before. The only problem with this approach is that you would have to accept a high percentage of failures, and this wouldn't come cheap as obviously studio costs would be very high. In the end, recording sessions stretched well into August and Island Records were, of course, getting worried about costs spiralling. Sheppard quotes an interview with Eno on his working method:

I used to book a different instrument each day. One day it would be a cello, another day a marimba, trombone … anything. I couldn't play any of them, but I just … as part of my kit, I would have a little idea I'd write for myself … 'Swing the microphone from the ceiling' and 'Hire a trombone'. So I've got two rules I'm going to use that day in the studio … and I'm going to try to make a piece of music.

Influenced by Krautrock artists such as Cluster, Eno also employed the use of drum machines, especially while working on simple two-note keyboard pieces that he could build up slowly when other musicians were not around; these pieces added a tranquil atmosphere to tracks and gave the album a very different feel than Eno's previous releases. In the end, more than 30 pieces of music were edited down to the 14 tracks that would make up the album with five vocal songs and nine instrumental pieces.

Eno: Another Green World (1975)

Personnel:
Brian Eno: guitar (snake, desert and digital), synthesizers, tapes, organ, piano, percussion, effects
Paul Rudolph: bass
Phil Collins: drums
Percy Jones: fretless bass
Rod Melvin: electric piano
Robert Fripp: guitar
John Cale: viola
Brian Turrington: bass, piano (track 13 only)
All songs written by Brian Eno
Produced by: Brian Eno and Rhett Davies
Cover by: Tom Phillips (front), Ritva Saarikko (back)
Recorded at: Island Studios
Released: 14 November 1975 (although yet again some release information says September)
Highest Chart Position: Did not chart in either the UK or US but reached number 24 in the charts in New Zealand
Tracklisting: Side One: 1. Sky Saw, 2. Over Fire Island, 3. St. Elmo's Fire, 4. In Dark Trees, 5. The Big Ship, 6. I'll Come Running, 7. Another Green World. Side Two: 1. Sombre Reptiles, 2. Little Fishes, 3. Golden Hours, 4. Becalmed, 5. Zawinul/Lava, 6. Everything Merges With The Night, 7. Spirits Drifting

Right from the very beginning, this was obviously a very different Eno that was being presented on this album. The cover painting, a detail from Tom Phillips's *After Raphael*, already gave the air of an art gallery to proceedings before the needle had even hit the vinyl. On the reverse, a photo of Eno now shorn of his long locks and glam rock image, sitting next to a pot plant thumbing his way through a book, looking every inch the quiet intellectual rather than the glamorous rock star of the last couple of years. The other thing of note was the track listing that revealed that four of the tracks were created by Eno alone without any other musicians. Eno continued to use the naming of his guitar sound to describe the vibe of his playing, and this can also be seen on previous albums, but here Eno outdid himself with this. Eno described the 'snake guitar' sound to *NME*'s Ian MacDonald in 1976:

> Snake guitar requires no particular skill … and essentially involves destroying the pitch element of the instrument in order to produce wedges of sound that can be used percussively or as a kind of punctuation.

And to Lester Bangs in *Musician* magazine in 1979:

> All those words are my descriptions of either a way of playing or a sound; in that case, it was because the kind of lines I was playing reminded me of the way a snake moves through the brush, a sort of speedy, forceful, liquid quality.

From the opening few seconds of 'Sky Saw', we are dealing with a very different beast than the previous album openers. Its angular guitars and Collins' and Jones' jazz-style rhythm section make for quite a jarring beginning, especially for an album that has some quite contemplative moods on it. Its lyrics are almost Dada-esque nonsense sung as two verses simultaneously over each other. It's an odd song that is part avant-rock and part Weather Report Jazz stylings – sections of it will be used on Eno's *Music For Films* album the following year – and the track ends with an almost classical refrain played by Cale on his viola. 'Over Fire Island' is a slight instrumental built around Jones's rubbery fretless bass and a steady percussion beat from Collins. Over the top of this, Eno plays some off-kilter and atonal notes on the synthesizers while echoed tape chirps warble beneath. This is music to conjure up an atmosphere of a place – the title suggests this – and we can all imagine this landscape without ever visiting the locale.

'St. Elmo's Fire' is one of the more straight-ahead rock/pop songs on the album, referencing a bizarre meteorological event where lightning seems to act in its own free will, 'licking up ropes and sweeping around propellers'. Accounts of this phenomenon are rare. The lyrics refer to a couple on some endless journey witnessing events through different landscapes until they reach a desert where they see St. Elmo's Fire 'Slitting ions in the ether' all under a blue August moon. Fripp's 'Wimshurst' guitar solo is a thing of beauty that takes the song in a different direction. The fact that only Fripp and Eno perform on this song shows how far their collaboration had come since *(No Pussyfooting)*. 'In Dark Trees' uses a drum machine put through a vast amount of echo as synths chug away in the background and Eno's guitar plays a mournful few notes over the top; this is the first of the most ambient-sounding pieces for the album.

'The Big Ship' uses a grandiose chord sequence over 'synthetic percussion', and it's here you can hear the influence of Krautrock bands like Cluster and even Kraftwerk in the way the track progresses. Next, Eno goes back to his rock song roots with 'I'll Come Running', a track that was used as a B side to his next 7" and was also recorded for a BBC radio session. Here Eno references older rock 'n' roll doo-wop songs musically, while the lyrics reference a lonely melancholia with Fripp's guitar lifting the track during its solo section over its odd rolling backing rhythm section. 'Another Green World' is an instrumental probably best known in the UK as the opening theme music for the BBC's arts television programme *Arena* with its piano fugue and five-note guitar riff and it closes side one.

Side two opens with 'Sombre Reptiles', another Eno-only instrumental that has strangely always reminded me of the US band The Residents. Its simple repeating guitar motif over a rolling percussion section creates a strange atmosphere. Oddly it would be a track performed by Manzanera and Eno's band 801 live the following year. 'Little Fishes' has an almost Japanese feel to its prepared piano and Farfisa organ as notes dart around like bright fishes in an ornamental garden pond.

'Golden Hours' is a song about privacy and pondering the meaning of existence, all the while whittling away the time with the visual landscape of television etc., that bombards us constantly in the modern world. Then Eno takes a reprieve and watches the sun slowly set over a landscape with a glass of wine in hand; these are the reflective moments that we have that can sometimes almost feel unreal as time seems to stand still. Its music is built around some punchy percussion organ chords, and again Fripp's guitar work takes the song into a different place while Cale's viola adds to the contemplative mood. Eno's vocals are double-tracked and again placed in some vast echo and reverb chamber. 'Becalmed' is a piano and synthesizer piece that would pre-date the sound used in the early eighties with Harold Budd and the kinds of atmosphere he would recycle for *Before And After Science*.

'Zawinul/Lava' is a track influenced/dedicated by jazz keyboard player Josef Zawinul with its chiming piano notes, its odd percussion and drifting guitar and bass sounds. 'Everything Merges With The Night' has a similar lyrical feel to 'On Some Faraway Beach' and even musically, it touches upon the earlier track. The words conjure up visions of landscapes by warm azure waters in some sub-tropical late summer afternoon. Eno's guitar holds notes almost endlessly, creating a wall of guitar sound that shimmers throughout the song and over Turrington's bass and piano. 'Spirits Drifting' is a slow ambient piece that hovers like summer heat in the air for the couple of minutes it exists and makes for an almost disquieting close to the album.

Critical reception for the album was overall fairly positive, some even claiming that it was Eno's best album to date. There were a few complaints in some papers about the lack of traditional rock songs on the album. Over the years, it has been generally recognised and re-evaluated as Eno's masterpiece and some even say that it's his definitive album. It was certainly the turning point of the old Eno into the new Brian Eno, both within the public and music press perceptions of the artist. Here Eno managed with one record to shake off his past and reinvent himself as an artist who views music more like experimental paintings; Eno became a landscape artist aurally, something that has remained with him ever since.

Before the album was released, Island would put out the 7" of a non-album track, a cover of the song 'The Lion Sleeps Tonight (Wimoweh)'. A fairly straightforward rendition of the 1961 song by Linda and Campbell and recorded by The Tokens, the song didn't trouble the charts and would certainly have been out of place on the album. Backed by 'I'll Come Running' it stands out as being a bit of an oddity even within Eno's seventies output.

It was also around the release of the album that Eno put forward the idea of creating a library label with Island that would put out modern classical experimental records that could be recorded cheaply and help expand not only the public's knowledge of the artists involved but also help represent Eno himself as some type of co-founder of experimental music by producing each album released. Strangely Island agreed to the idea and the Obscure Records label was born. Island put out these albums at a budget price and used them as a kind of 'shop window' for helping buyers to discover other Island artists at the same time. Eno cherry-picked some of his favourite modern composers and each release had a uniform cover with a different area of it highlighted in colour. Eno designed these sleeves himself and Island pencilled in four initial releases to see if there would be any interest in this sort of thing.

Island released the first four albums simultaneously to cut costs on promotion for each release. The first of these in 1975 was 'Obscure no.1', which was Gavin Bryars' album *The Sinking Of The Titanic*, an orchestral piece first performed in 1972 which took up the entire first side of the vinyl album, while the second was consumed with Bryars' work 'Jesus' Blood Never Failed Me', produced of course by Eno and Rhett Davies at Island's Basing Street Studios.

Eno's own contribution was on 'Obscure no.3' and was the bestselling of all the releases on the label. This was his first recording after discovering ambient music after his accident and took up one whole side of the vinyl release. It was titled 'Discreet Music' and was about to have a profound influence on one of his colleagues as it was placed on repeated listening by David Bowie holed up in his LA home on a cocktail of cocaine and milk. It was also the first album to use Eno's first name on its sleeve and thus another turning point for him in 1975.

Brian Eno: Discreet Music (1975)

Personnel:
Brian Eno: synthesizer (with digital recall system, effects graphic equalizer, echo unit, delay), tape
The Cockpit Ensemble (conducted and arranged by Gavin Bryars)
All songs written by Brian Eno
Produced by: Brian Eno
Recorded at: Eno's Studio and Trident Studio
Highest Chart Position: –
Tracklisting: Side One: 1. Discreet Music, Side Two: 1. Three Variations On The Canon In D Major By Johann Pachelbel

'Discreet Music' is a 30-minute piece that owes nothing to rock 'n' roll but hints at modern classical work, mainly minimalism. Oddly the track is too long for one side of vinyl, as most vinyl lengths are approximately 25 minutes at maximum. The other thing about 'Discreet Music' is the fact that the track slowly fades in and out, making it sound like it could go on forever and we are only hearing a snippet of the recording (which, in fact, we were). The sound has an almost soporific effect on the listener as its notes fade up and out during its running time. The piece creates its own environment in many ways, as even though it is a piece of ambient music, it somehow takes command of the room it is playing in. Its simplicity is the thing that works in its favour, as after a while, you almost stop listening to the notes and just wallow in its atmosphere. The album sleeve also contains a diagram on how Eno created this piece of music.

Side two of the album is a totally different beast altogether. Eno had come up with the idea of deconstructing one of his favourite pieces of classical music. Eno took the score and started overlaying permutations on each piece that would not appear in the original manuscript. Eno describes something of the making of this on the sleeve notes for the album:

Another way of satisfying the interest in self-regulating and self-generating systems is exemplified in the three variations on the Pachelbel Canon … In this case, the 'system' is a group of performers with a set of instructions and the 'input' is the fragment of Pachelbel. Each variation takes a small section of the score (two or four bars) as its starting point and permutates the players' parts such that they overlay each other in ways not suggested in the original score.

Eno gave these parts very typical tongue-in-cheek names that were taken from an inaccurate translation of the original titles on the back of an LP (but one feels also modified by Eno). They are 'Fullness Of Wind', 'French Catalogues' and 'Brutal Ardour'. Bryars seems to have been mainly in control of the piece, with Eno adding 'lots of reverb' in the studio consol. Eno later admitted that he didn't think the experiment was very successful and when the album was finally released on CD many years later, he inserted a whole minute's worth of silence between the title track and the Canon as if in a way of separating them aurally or so that the listener had plenty of time to switch the CD off if they needed too. When the album was originally released it was sold at the discount price of £1.99 to try and draw people in to not only buying this but also the other Obscure releases.

Eno, though, had one more album to release before the closing of the year and these were the recordings he made with Fripp during the spring, and the last album by them as a duo to appear for many years. The album featured a photo taken backstage by Antonio Tiedra at one of their concerts and showed Eno in the final stages of his long-haired glam rock glory. *Evening Star* also featured a glorious front cover painting by Peter Schmidt featuring a warm, tranquil sunset haze over what looks like an island. The cover sums up well the kind of music that could be found when you placed your needle on the disc and was an excellent visual representation of the sound the duo were making.

Fripp & Eno: Evening Star (1975)
Personnel:
Robert Fripp: guitar
Brian Eno: loops and synthesizer
Produced by: Eno and Fripp
Recorded at: Eno's Studio, Olympic Studios, AIR Studios and Live at the Paris Olympia
Released: December 1975
Tracklisting: Side One: 1. Wind On Water, 2. Evening Star, 3. Evensong, 4. Wind On Wind, Side Two: 1. An Index Of Metals

'Wind On Water' shimmers like a summer heat haze with Fripp's guitar tapping adding layers of undulating sound over Eno's tape loops. It does conjure the vision of a gentle sea breeze on a warm day and is some of Fripp's most subtle guitar work. The track slowly fades into the chord structure of 'Evening Star', possibly the highlight track of the duo's partnership. Fripp's cello-like glissandi guitar plays gently over Eno's hovering synth motif to give an amazing breath of sound that remains constantly interesting as it changes over the track. It is ambient music that flows mercurially and never turns into bland New Age music.

'Evensong' is a slight piece that loops around itself and sounds almost like a lullaby in comparison to the previous tracks, and Fripp's guitar is elegantly simple. 'Wind On Wind' was a section taken from Eno's *Discreet Music* and was part of the original tape that Eno sent to Fripp.

The second side of the album is totally taken up with a 28-minute drone piece called 'An Index Of Metals' where e-guitar notes are looped on themselves, with distortion being slowly added to some of the loops as the track progresses. This gives an almost jarring and disquieting feel to the piece making it feel quite uncomfortable in places. In a strange way the piece feels like an abstract painting, both beautiful and indecipherable at the same time but with a certain nervous energy from its creator.

Before the album was released, Fripp had already announced that he would be retiring from music to focus on spiritual pursuits instead. In truth, his retirement would only last two years when he was coerced back into the studio by Peter Gabriel and later by Eno as well.

For Eno, this had been a tumultuous but also productive year where he had managed to create a career-defining album and had also discovered a music sound that has occupied him ever since. He would be stepping into the new year totally transformed from the Eno that started 1975.

Intermission: Eno As Producer And Session Player

It is at this halfway point that it is worth discussing some of the other musical projects that Eno was involved in during the seventies, mainly as a producer but sometimes as a session musician as well. To cover all these releases in-depth in the main narrative would take up too much space so a brief discussion of these can be found below; also I will not be covering them in quite chronological order but by artist and/or label.

One of his earliest post-Roxy credits was in 1974 as a synthesizer player on sometimes Hawkwind vocalist Robert Calvert's first album *Captain Lockheed And The Starfighters*, a kind of Monty Python-esque concept album. It was also when working on this album that Eno met Paul Rudolph, who featured quite heavily on Eno's seventies solo releases. Eno was called back a year later to produce Calvert's follow-up album *Lucky Leif And The Longships*, both of these albums being released on United Artists Records.

However, in 1973 Eno completed his first work outside of Roxy Music, producing and playing on the album *Portsmouth Sinfonia – Plays Popular Classics*. Additionally, Eno wrote the sleeve notes for this release on Transatlantic Records. He later produced and played clarinet on the Sinfonia's second album in 1974, *Hallelujah*. Also, in 1974 Eno added 'Enosification' to two tracks on progressive rock band Genesis's sixth studio album *The Lamb Lies Down On Broadway*.

In 1975 Eno also added vocals, synthesizer and treatments to Phil Manzanera's *Diamond Head* album, and the results from these recording sessions would be were that Manzanera would form his own band 801 for live dates in 1976 and Eno featured on synthesizer on the band's debut studio album in 1977 called *Listen Now*.

In 1974 Eno provided synthesizer for Andy MacKay's first solo album *In Search Of Eddie Riff,* which also featured 801's Lloyd Watson and Eno's Roxy replacement Eddie Jobson (one assumes that they were not in the studio at the same time). Eno had also co-written the song 'Time Regained' that appeared on the B side of MacKay's first solo 7 inch. In addition, the track does not appear on the original vinyl pressings of the album in 1974.

In 1976 Eno was called in to produce the new Island label signing Ultravox! Featuring original vocalist John Foxx. Ultravox! were actually the perfect band for Eno to produce, mixing as they did, an early Roxy Music glam experimental sound with new wave-type guitars and Krautrock synthesizer passages influenced by Kraftwerk. In Sheppard's book, Foxx describes working with Eno:

Eno was very low-key and practical. We played through some songs, which he recorded on a Dictaphone. He liked what he heard. Then said he'd check record company arrangements re: finances et cetera, and get back to us. Next thing, the studio is booked and we were off ... Basically, we played what we'd rehearsed. Back behind the glass, Brian either accepted or adjusted, mostly accepted; then he and we worked on the sonic layout. It was all very amicable.

Foxx later went on to a solo career, part of which included making a series of ambient albums very much influenced by Eno's work.

Eno also added his synth work to a track on progressive rock band Camel's 1977 album *Rain Dances*; this was a flute-driven atmospheric piece called 'Elke' that certainly has more than a touch of Eno's atmospherics going on.

Eno's probably best-known production work (and also synth playing and backing vocals) was on the two 1978 albums by Talking Heads. *Fear Of Music* and *More Songs About Buildings And Food* established the US new wave band as art rockers with an element of funk and were the records that forged their career and kick-started a lifelong friendship between Eno and singer/guitarist David Byrne that led to the influential album the duo would make in 1981 *My Life In The Bush Of Ghosts*.

Other US acts produced by Eno in 1978 were the first album by the band Devo, an act that Eno and David Bowie had witnessed live together. Eno produced their album at Conny Plank's studio in Cologne, Germany, the place where many famous Krautrock bands had so far been recorded, and the album called *Q: Are We Not Men? A: We Are Devo!* was released on 15 September 1978. Eno also produced a compilation album by 'no wave' American punk bands such as the infamous Lydia Lunch's band, Teenage Jesus And The Jerks, called *No New York*. This was released in America only on the Antilles label and became a sought-after item in the early eighties.

However, Eno's biggest production duties were with the already mentioned Obscure Label, that released ten albums between 1975 and 1978. These are listed in order here:

Obscure no 1: Gavin Bryars – The Sinking Of The Titanic (1975)
Obscure no 2: Christopher Hobbs, John Adams, Gavin Bryars – Ensemble Pieces (1975)
Obscure no 3: Brian Eno – Discreet Music (1975)

Obscure no 4: David Toop and Max Eastley – New and Rediscovered Musical Instruments (1975)
Obscure no 5: Jan Steele and John Cage – Voices And Instruments (1976)
Obscure no 6: Michael Nyman – Decay Music (1976)
Obscure no 7: The Penguin Café Orchestra – Music From The Penguin Café (1976)
Obscure no 8: John White and Gavin Bryars – Machine Music (1978)
Obscure no 9: Tom Phillips and Gavin Bryars – Irma (1978)
Obscure no 10: Harold Budd – The Pavilion Of Dreams (1978)

Most of these albums have now become quite sought-after, especially Nyman's, who would find fame later for his Peter Greenaway film scores and Harold Budd's first-ever album. Budd would make two exquisite albums with Eno in the early eighties and one of them, *The Plateaux Of Mirror*, would be part of Eno's 'ambient label' series of releases.

The music on these albums is a mixture of avant-garde and experimental classical music, with some, like Budd's and Nyman's, hinting at ambient music but most borrowing or at least referencing ideas from Cage and Cardew. The one big abnormality here is The Penguin Café Orchestra, whose album mixes string quartet sounds with electric guitars, to make it the most easily accessible musical hybrid in the collection. The band went on to produce many recordings and live performances until the passing of its leader Simon Jeffes in 1997.

The Year with Swollen Soundtracks 1976

1976 was the year that Eno almost disappeared from view in comparison to the previous four years, with only two album credits to his name (one even being a live album), and it would seem that he had slightly run out of steam compared to three album releases over the space of two months in 1975. However, 1976 was the year that started perhaps Eno's most important collaboration of the seventies, and for many, it will be some of the work he is best known for, even though his name doesn't feature as the lead artist on the front covers.

The year started with Eno being approached by film director Derek Jarman about creating a soundtrack for his new film *Sebastiane*. Jarman had already made several video short films and had worked as set designer on director Ken Russell's film *The Devils*. *Sebastiane* was a homoerotic film based on the martyrdom in the third century of Saint Sebastian and the entire dialogue of the film would be delivered in dog or slang Latin; it was the only British film ever to be issued with English subtitles.

Eno was thrilled to be asked to participate, seeing this as an opportunity to break into the fairly lucrative work of film soundtracks. Eno got out his trusty VCS3 and began putting together a series of drones and slow, meditative pieces swathed in reverb that would augment the visual aspects of the film rather than detract from it. As the budget for the film was very small, Eno only asked for a tiny fee for his work, realising this could kick-start a whole new way of bringing his minimalist music études to a different audience; in fact, he had already been asked to provide some sounds for a theatre production of Alan Drury's play *Sparrowfall*.

Working on these pieces, Eno formulated the idea of creating a library album full of themes that could be used on potential soundtracks in the future. These recordings could be handed to potential film companies and filmmakers as an introduction of the kind of sounds that Eno could provide for their work. It consisted of a series of short vignettes that gave a flavour of Eno's soundscapes at that moment in time. Apart from some new compositions, he recycled some of the unused recordings from the making of *Another Green World* to tidy up any loose ends from the previous year with the potential of earning back some of the money from the protracted studio time it took to make the album.

For the second time, Eno's name was preceded by his first name on a record. The album was released in a limited edition of just 500 copies, many of which were distributed to production companies. The album was finally released to the general public in 1978 with a slightly different track order to that of the original limited edition release. As it is officially a 1976 release, here are its details:

Brian Eno: Music For Films (1976)

Personnel:
Brian Eno: synthesizer, tapes, treatments, guitar
Percy Jones: bass
Phil Collins: drums
Paul Rudolph: guitar
Bill MacCormick: bass
Dave Mattacks: percussion
Fred Frith: electric guitar
Robert Fripp: guitar
John Cale: viola
Rod Melvin: electric piano
Rhett Davies: trumpet
All songs written by Brian Eno
Produced by: Brian Eno
Recorded at: Basing Street Studios
Highest Chart Position: –
Tracklisting: Side One: 1. M386, 2. Aragon, 3. From The Same Hill, 4. Inland Sea, 5. Two Rapid Formations, 6. Slow Water, 7. Sparrowfall 1–3, Side Two: 1. Quartz, 2. Events In Dense Fog, 3. There Is Nobody, 4. A Measured Room, 5. Patrolling Wire Borders, 6. Task Force, 7. Alternative 3, 8. Strange Light, 9. Final Sunset

The original limited album included the tracks 'Becalmed', 'Spain', 'Untitled', 'The Last Door', 'Chemin De Fer', 'Evening Star', 'Another Green World', 'In Dark Trees', 'Melancholy Waltz', 'From The Coast', 'Shell', 'Little Fishes', 'Empty Landscape', 'Reactor', 'The Secret', 'Marseilles' and 'Juliet'. So in many respects a very different album than the 1978 official/general release with a lot more already available pieces of music included in it.

For the 1978 re-issue of the album, Eno rearranged tracks into what he felt was a better running order and one that would be easier for the general listener to consume. Many of the pieces featured last under two minutes in duration and are very slight atmospherics that bubble up and disappear again just as quickly. Some are selections from the *Sebastiane* soundtrack, but these pieces were renamed for the 1978 album. These are all mood pieces and their atmosphere changes from track to track. As an album, it's a slightly disappointing affair because as you settle into one mood piece, it has gone in the ether so quickly to be replaced by something different. In a strange way, the record is more of a sampler album and should be viewed as such when listening to it. As many pieces would end up being used for movies and TV documentaries over the following year, it provided both Eno and EG with a steady income over a long period of time. Eno explained to *Mojo* magazine's Andy Gill:

One of them has been used 25 times in different TV programmes. It's about 30 seconds long and it took me 30 seconds to make.

During the long, hot British summer of 1976, Eno busied himself, first of all with producing more artists for the Obscure label (discussed in the previous chapter), and by also helping out his old friend Phil Manzanera on some recordings that creatively had seemed to stall in the Basing Street Studios. It was at this point that Manzanera decided to form his own art rock band to take his compositions on the road and named them 801 after the line in the song he co-wrote with Eno called 'The True Wheel'. In July, Manzanera set about recruiting and rehearsing a band which would, of course, include Eno, ready to take on some possibly extensive gigging. The band would be a supergroup and included an eclectic array of musicians to bring to life the songs. The line-up brought together Curved Air's Francis Monkman, Quiet Sun's Bill MacCormick, session drummer Simon Phillips and old friend Lloyd Watson on second guitar.

Intensive rehearsals began at Island's rehearsal rooms in Hammersmith, with Eno pushing for a certain amount of experimentation and, of course, fun to proceedings. Eno also managed to take on board a large amount of the singing duties with the band, as at least three of his compositions were going to be performed during the band's set. During rehearsals, Watson struggled with some of the complex time signatures for some of Manzanera's tracks but eventually nailed them after rehearsing for three weeks solid.

The tour started at the least rock 'n' roll venue ever, at Norfolk's West Runton Pavilion, which was more used to holding ballroom dancing rather than avant-rock bands. Then the band headed for what was one of the biggest rock events during the seventies and early eighties, the

Reading Rock Festival, which in typical festival fashion, was rained out after Britain had been scorching for weeks in a record-breaking heatwave. 801 were situated between the prog rock behemoths of Van Der Graaf Generator and Camel, and it was here that Eno presented his new image to a large rock crowd, still with a smattering of make-up. He wore the more sober black jeans and T-shirt making him look like a bookish artist rather than the glamorous rock star. Eno introduced 'Third Uncle' as 'the fastest song ever written', and the set also included 'The Fat Lady of Limbourg'. Many songs would not make the final live album release, so renditions of 'I'll Come Running' and 'Golden Hours' are now lost in the ether.

801's performance was noted as being one of the highlights of the festival and the band were scheduled to do some European dates, but after a riot at a festival in Orange, the French government banned all future events. So, Island Records hastily arranged a gig at London's Queen Elizabeth Hall and decided that they would try and capture the band's performance that night. The recordings were finally released in November 1976, but by that point, the band were no more and these would be Eno's last live performances of the seventies. Island would place a full-page advert in the music press for the album with the headline 'That's All Folks!' also saying that 'On Thursday 3 September a group called 801 played their third and last gig'. The advert gives a résumé of each of the band members with a large photo of them in the middle.

801: 801 Live (1976)

Personnel:
Phil Manzanera: guitar
Eno: synthesizer, guitar, tapes, vocals
Bill MacCormick: bass, vocals
Simon Phillips: drums
Francis Monkman: electric piano, clavinet
Lloyd Watson: slide Guitar, vocals
Engineer: Rhett Davies
Recorded: Live at the Queen Elizabeth Hall, 3 September 1976
Released: November 1976
Highest Chart Position: –
Tracklisting: Side One: 1. Lagrima (Manzanera), 2. TNK (Lennon/McCartney), 3. East Of Asteroid (MacCormick, Manzanera), 4. Rongwrong (Hayward), 5. Sombre Reptiles (Eno). Side Two: 1. Baby's On Fire (Eno), 2. Diamond

Head (Manzanera), 3. Miss Shapiro (Eno, Manzanera), 4. You Really Got Me
(Davies), 5. Third Uncle (Eno)

As live albums go, *801* is a good testament to what the band sounded
like at the time. The most surprising thing was the cover versions that
the band decided to use, The Beatles' 'Tomorrow Never Knows' (listed as
TNK) and The Kinks' 'You Really Got Me', which were already becoming
rock standard cover songs by this point. 801 turned the Lennon song
into an avant-funk number with Eno's voice perfectly suited to the
otherworldly lyrics and Manzanera working the fret board hard. 'You
Really Got Me' turns into a proto-punk anthem with Eno's bleeping VCS3
underpinning his vocals, and Manzanera's guitar break almost turns the
song into heavy metal overload.

'Third Uncle' is played at an even faster tempo than on the *Taking
Tiger...* album, but apart from that is a pretty faithful version with Phillip's
drumming going into override. 'Baby's On Fire' is offered a slightly
funkier beat with Eno's vocals being both sneering and tuneful and is a
fantastic performance, and Manzanera didn't try to copy Fripp and made
the guitar solo his own.

'Diamond Head' is a laid-back mood piece where the band get a chance
to break away from some of the more frenetic numbers. 'Miss Shapiro''s
big riff gets a slightly heavier treatment and Eno's vocals are again
perfect, which makes you realise just what a good live singer he was
and makes it an extra shame he abandoned live performance for over
a decade. 'Sombre Reptiles' is given a slightly more dub element in its
rhythm section, especially in MacCormick's bass and Monkman's choppy
keyboard stabs.

In 2012 a double album was released of *801 Live,* which included the
original record plus a second one recorded at rehearsals at Shepperton
Studios on 23 August 1976. The annoying thing about this is that it
replicates the same track listing as the live album, so we don't get to hear
some of the other pieces that the band performed and rehearsed at the
time; this makes it a rather frustrating release as these extra songs would
have made this double album a must-have for any Eno/Roxy etc. collector.

By the end of September, Eno was on his way to Germany to meet up with
the band Harmonia at their studio in Forst to work on some improvised
recordings with Dieter Moebius, Hans-Joachim Roedelius and Michael
Rother of the band. These recordings began to point Eno in another
direction as he immersed himself in the sounds coming out of the alternative

rock scene in Germany. Eno had already talked to Roedelius 18 months earlier after seeing the band perform live, and contacting him again, took up the invitation to travel over to work with him and the rest of the band.

Harmonia's studio was located on the edge of a forest and with very few people around for miles, it was a calm and relaxing place away from it all where Eno could meditate on the last four years as well as having the right ambience to create new low event horizon music with the band. He lived commune-style with the others and they worked whenever the mood took them, with Eno saying they 'came up with tons of stuff'. Sheppard interviewed Roedelius:

Brian fitted right into our community and the way we worked in our ad hoc studio. He lived with us in our part of the old house where our community lived. He often took care of our daughter, came with us for shopping or went with me to the forest. I bought him tools to cut wood with me. He shared our family life.

It's hard to imagine the urbane Eno of the seventies leading a rural lifestyle away from the trappings of galleries, experimental music concerts and most of all, glamorous model-type women. The music that they recorded that late summer of 1976 would take over 20 years to finally see a release and then only in a truncated form; it was only in 2016 that an expanded version of the album on double vinyl would finally see the light of day under the name *Harmonia & Eno '76 – Tracks and Traces*.

Harmonia & Eno '76: Tracks And Traces (released 2016)

Performer, producer, written by: Brian Eno, Dieter Moebius, Hans-Joachim Roedelius, Michael Rother
Recorded at: Harmonia Studio, Forst, September 1976
Released by: Grönland Records, Germany
Highest Chart Position: –
Tracklisting: Side One: 1. Welcome, 2. Atmosphere, 3. Vamos Companeros, 4. By The Riverside, Side Two: 1. Luneburg Heath, 2. Sometimes In Autumn, Side Three: 1. Weird Dream, 2. Almost, Side Four: 1. Les Demoiselles, 2. When Shade Was Born, 3. Trace, 4. Aubade

It's odd to think why these recordings took so long to be released and even then, these seem like a semi-official release even though they have been remastered. They also feel like a very different beast than the Cluster & Eno albums that were released in 1977 with ostensibly the same line-up minus Rother. Eno has one vocal performance on the track 'Luneburg Heath' and this particular piece feels more like an Eno solo track. Eno had deliberately left his Oblique Strategies cards at home so that the recordings would not have the influence of his Zen-like wisdom dictating them. The songs are a mixed bunch of almost avant-garde experimental pieces and the quieter, drifting ambient tracks. Even though these are edited, it is easy to see that these are largely jamming-style improvisations, with some pieces losing a sense of clarity and others sitting oddly next to each other in the final running order. No surprise that it is the quieter works that seem to create a more interesting atmosphere and possibly where Eno's influence is greatest. These are an interesting snapshot of Eno in 1976 and also, you can begin to see the influence of these artists that will seep its way onto Eno's next solo album.

When Eno arrived back in the UK, he was waylaid by a young musician called Dennis Leigh, who had changed his name to John Foxx and was now lead singer of an electronic punk band called Ultravox! The band had just signed to Island Records on the strength of their live shows and were in the process of beginning to record their debut album, which mixed Kraftwerk and The New York Dolls in an odd brewing pot that had not been witnessed since Roxy's debut. Eno, who sat in on a rehearsal, was very interested and became the producer along with Steve Lillywhite for the album. Eno brought in his Oblique Strategies and lots of conceptual ideas that the band could if they wished, add to the already heady mix of songs they had written. It was with this album that Eno would show himself as a proper 'rock' producer for other artists as he coerced better performances from the band than the original song structures.

It was near the end of the recording sessions that Eno took an important phone call from David Bowie asking Eno for his assistance for some recordings he was making in France. Bowie said he wasn't sure at this stage if the recordings would be released or not, but that left it open for both artists to experiment. Foxx told Sheppard in an interview what exactly happened:

> It was quite funny, really, because Brian went all coy; wasn't sure if he should really do it and so on. We all howled, 'Go on Brian, you have to.' Of course, he was just showing off by playing hard to get. It was endearing, really.

The offer came as no surprise, really, as Eno had attended the new Bowie 'Thin White Duke' persona at one of the shows he played at his Empire Pool Wembley residency the previous May. Eno was much taken with Bowie's new glacial *Station To Station* sound and reacquainted himself with Bowie backstage at the show, where The Duke admitted to Eno that he had constantly been spinning *Discreet Music* on his turntable.

Bowie by this point, was also coming to the end of what was a nightmare time in LA (on a diet of cocaine, eggs and capsicums) and wanted to reacquaint himself with Europe and new European music to escape his own self-destructive lifestyle. Bowie, dragging along fellow drug casualty Iggy Pop, relocated to Berlin in an attempt to sort themselves out, and hopefully feel inspired to start creating a new form of music and for Bowie to reinvent himself yet again in the public eye, hopefully discarding his 'drug-addled rock star' image that being in America had created for him. In July 1976, Bowie headed to the north-west suburbs of Paris to Le Château d'Hérouville studio to start work on Iggy's debut solo album *The Idiot*. When this was completed, Bowie decided to return to the studio later and fiddle around with some rejected instrumental pieces he had written for the soundtrack of his film *The Man Who Fell To Earth* (1976) and also set about writing some new songs with a definite eye on a change of style musically and towards his own future.

Bowie's working title for the album was *New Music, Night and Day and* it was only later in the recording process that the name of the album would change to *Low*. Bowie then contacted his usual producer Tony Visconti to come and spend a month with him and Eno recording, and in a three-way telephone conversation, Bowie asked what he could bring to the table. Hugo Wilcken discusses the conversation in his 2005 book *Low*:

Bowie asked Visconti what he thought he could contribute to the sessions; Visconti mentioned the pitch-shifting Eventide Harmonizer he'd just got, Bowie asked what it did, and Visconti famously replied that 'it fucks with the fabric of time!' Bowie was delighted, and Eno went berserk. He said, 'We've got to have it!'

Sessions begin with bass player George Murray and drummer Dennis Davis laying down an initial backing track which took only five days and by the time Eno arrived at the studio, both Murray and Davis had already departed. Eno's main role at this point was to oversee and participate in overdubbing musical ideas that Bowie and his band had almost completed for side one of the album. Eno and Bowie had already discussed that side two would be entirely instrumental and have a more electronic and ambient flavour than the song-based side one. Eno brought along his trusty EMS synth so that he could process some of the sounds created by Carlos Alomar's guitar through it, just as he had done for Manzanera in Roxy Music. Eno would sometimes be left alone in the studio to lay down a sonic bed of sounds. Hugo Wilcken quotes from an interview with Eno:

> I was trying to give some kind of sonic character to the track, so the thing had a distinct textural feel that gave it a mood to begin with … It's hard to describe that because it was never the same twice, and it's not susceptible to description very easily in ordinary music terms. It would just be doing the thing that you can do with tape so that you can treat the music as malleable.

Eno had also convinced Bowie to use Oblique Strategies during the recording so that new ideas could be thrown in randomly and thus change the direction and sound of songs Bowie had already recorded before Eno's arrival, although guitarist Carlos Alomar found the cards a distraction and felt they were taking the music away from a pure sound and making it somehow more machine-like. Bowie was already a good improviser – most of the songs on *Low* came out of improvisations – but the cards not only added an extra focus for him but also the chance of a random entity working within a track's favour. Eno and Bowie would discuss endlessly different musical directions as well as about European experimental avant-garde classical music during the sessions for the album.

While the album was being recorded, Bowie had to return to Paris for four days to attend court proceedings against his manager Michael Lippman. Eno seeing an empty paid-for studio going to waste, decided he would start working on a new piece of music, and if Bowie liked the piece, then he could have it for his album and if he didn't, Eno would pay him for the studio time and use the track on his own next solo album. The track that Eno worked on was probably *Low*'s most downbeat, melancholic and disturbing track, later named by Bowie as 'Warszawa'. Sheppard quotes from an interview with Visconti about the making of the track:

> Side two starts out with my son Delaney who was about four years old at the time, but who's a fairly good piano player, just going 'da, da, da, da,

da, da'. Brian had developed an affection for the little boy, and was in the same room, and he said, 'Wait a minute,' pushed Delaney off the piano, and used that 'da, da, da' as the first notes of side two, the first three notes of 'Warszawa'.

Eno would layer the track with synth sounds along with a string keyboard called a Chamberlin, which was the precursor of the Mellotron , an instrument that was ubiquitous on progressive rock records in the seventies. Eno, though, uses it for a section of haunted chord sequences that pop up throughout the track giving it an eerie and detached feeling. During Bowie's absence, he also worked on building up instrumentation on a notebook idea that Bowie had called 'Art Decade', fledging the random few notes into a proper piece of music.

When Bowie returned from his sojourn in Paris, Eno played him 'Warszawa' and Bowie was immediately taken with the track and went into the microphone booth to record a wordless vocal motif over the last part of the song adding to the strange sound of the piece. The rest of side two of the album took less than two weeks to complete in the studio, using some extracts from Bowie's *Man Who Fell To Earth* pieces to fill out some of the songs. Now all Bowie had to do was convince his record company RCA to release their hard work, which he had already surmised wouldn't be an easy task due to the nature of the tracks he was presenting to them.

Right: Eno in his full glam glory in late 1972. Images like this would be used for magazine posters.

Below: Eno onstage with Roxy Music in 1972. His image would get more flamboyant with each tour.

Left: The cover for the first Roxy Music album 1972, designed by Bryan Ferry and featuring the first of many 'Roxy' girls, Kari-Ann Muller. (*Island/Reprise*)

栄光のロキシー伝説はこの2曲のシングルの相次ぐ大ヒットから始まった！ —今野雄二— ILR-10769 STEREO

ヴァージニア・プレイン
・パジャマラマ

Virginia Plain·Pyjamarama

Roxy Music

＊ロキシー・ミュージック

Right: Japanese picture sleeve 7" with alternate Kari-Ann photo for the release of the first two singles packaged together in 1974.

Roxy Music
pyjamarama

Left: The Italian picture sleeve for the Roxy single 'Pyjamarama' in 1973. This was a gatefold cover and is now hard to find.

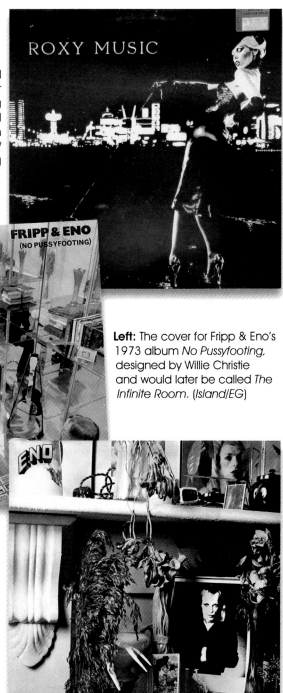

Right: The cover for the second Roxy Music album *For Your Pleasure* (1973) featuring Amanda Lear who would introduce the band on stage on the tour for the album. (*Island/ Warner Bros*)

Left: The cover for Fripp & Eno's 1973 album *No Pussyfooting,* designed by Willie Christie and would later be called *The Infinite Room.* (*Island/EG*)

Right: Eno's first solo album *Here Come the Warm Jets* (1974). The photo was taken at his flat by Lorenz Zatecky and features the saucy playing card. (*Island*)

Left: A Roxy publicity shot from 1973 taken on their final tour with Eno, probably taken backstage at *The Old Grey Whistle Test* performance.

Right: Roxy having fun recording the first album at Command Studios in March 1972.

Above: Roxy recording *For Your Pleasure* at Air Studios in February 1973 with producer Chris Thomas.

Right: A Japanese advert for *For Your Pleasure* with Eno's photo larger than the others. This was the type of thing that annoyed Bryan Ferry and helped lead to Eno's departure.

Left: Eno's second album *Taking Tiger Mountain by Strategy* (1974), with a lithographed cover by Peter Schmidt. (*Island*)

Right: Japanese insert with alternate design for the *Taking Tiger Mountain by Strategy* album in 1974.

Left: 1975's *Another Green World* showing a detail of the Tom Philips painting 'After Raphael'. (*Island*)

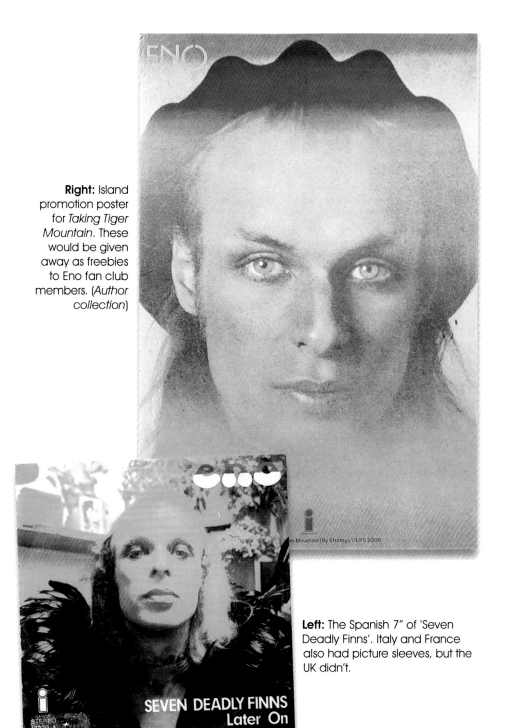

Right: Island promotion poster for *Taking Tiger Mountain*. These would be given away as freebies to Eno fan club members. (*Author collection*)

Left: The Spanish 7" of 'Seven Deadly Finns'. Italy and France also had picture sleeves, but the UK didn't.

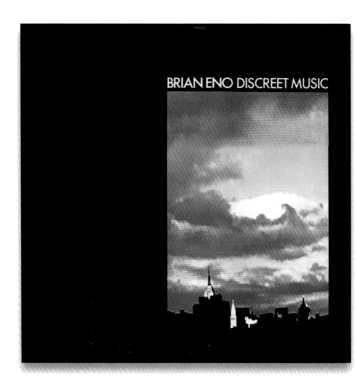

BRIAN ENO DISCREET MUSIC

Left: Cover for the reissue of the album *Discreet Music* from 1975 on Eno's own imprint label Obscure Records. (*Obscure*)

Right: Peter Schmidt's painting adorns the cover of Fripp & Eno's *Evening Star* album from 1975. The painting was originally created in 1970. (*Island*)

EVENING STAR FRIPP & ENO

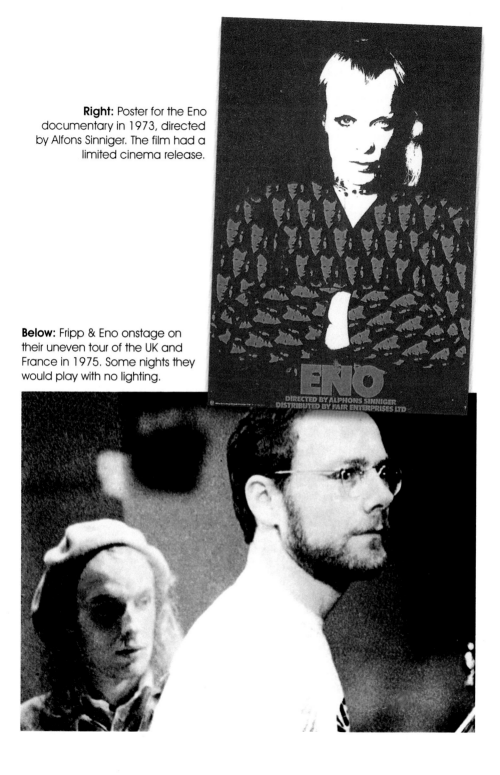

Right: Poster for the Eno documentary in 1973, directed by Alfons Sinniger. The film had a limited cinema release.

Below: Fripp & Eno onstage on their uneven tour of the UK and France in 1975. Some nights they would play with no lighting.

ENO

DIRECTED BY ALPHONS SINNIGER
DISTRIBUTED BY FAIR ENTERPRISES LTD

MUSIC FOR FILMS   BRIAN ENO

Left: The minimalist
cover design for the
1978 reissue of *Music
for Films*. The original
1976 cover had the
EG logo and address
on the front. (*EG*)

Right: The *801
Live* album was
photographed by
Richard Wallis at
Queen Elizabeth Hall,
London, in 1976.
(*Island*)

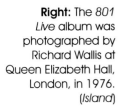

PHIL MANZANERA
ENO
BILL MacCORMICK
FRANCIS MONKMAN
SIMON PHILLIPS
LLOYD WATSON

801
Live

Harmonia & Eno '76
Tracks and Traces *reissue*

Right: Even though the recordings were made in 1976, the *Harmonia & Eno* album was not officially released for more than 20 years later. (*Groenland*)

Left: David Bowie's 1977 album *Low* with its cover taken from the film *The Man Who Fell to Earth* (1975). Eno features prominently on side two. (*RCA*)

Above: Fripp, Visconti, Bowie and Eno sharing a joke at Hansa by The Wall studios in Berlin in July 1977.

Below: Eno being interviewed at Island offices in 1978, pondering his next move. (*Chalkie Davies*)

Right: Eno in a publicity shot for *Before And After Science* in 1977 taken by his then partner Ritva Saarikko.

Left: Eno & Schmidt with the limited free prints given away with first pressings of *Before And After Science* on the wall behind them. (*Ritva Saarikko*)

Left: Cover for 1977's *Cluster & Eno* with a photograph taken by Cluster. This album would be a Germany-only release. (*Sky*)

Right: Bowie's iconic cover for 1977's *Heroes* album, based on a painting by Erich Heckel called 'Roquairol'. (*RCA*)

Left: The glam days are now gone, and a new arty Eno emerges from Ritva Saarikko's cover photo of 1977's *Before And After Science*. (*Polydor*)

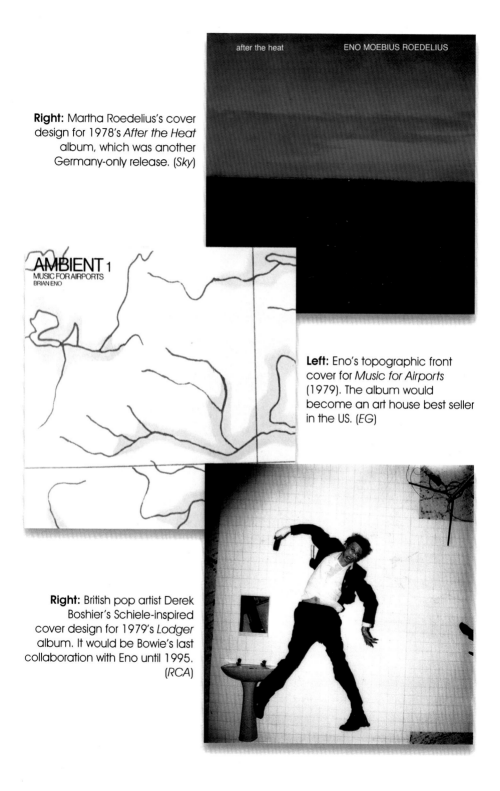

after the heat   ENO MOEBIUS ROEDELIUS

Right: Martha Roedelius's cover design for 1978's *After the Heat* album, which was another Germany-only release. (*Sky*)

AMBIENT 1
MUSIC FOR AIRPORTS
BRIAN ENO

Left: Eno's topographic front cover for *Music for Airports* (1979). The album would become an art house best seller in the US. (*EG*)

Right: British pop artist Derek Boshier's Schiele-inspired cover design for 1979's *Lodger* album. It would be Bowie's last collaboration with Eno until 1995. (*RCA*)

"ENOVATIONS"

Newsletter Summer '79

Left: The cover for the Summer 1979 issue of Enovations the newsletter/fanzine made by EG Management and featuring Peter Schmidt's unused cover painting for Before and After Science.

情 景 浮 遊

環境からの誘惑に静かに身を委ねる事の楽しさ。
――溶け込むか、取り込むか――

オン・ランド／ブライアン・イーノ

obscure ブライアン・イーノが設立した新鋭、実験音楽のレーベル
オブスキュア・レーベル

Right: A Japanese promotional flyer for *Music for Airports* using a Ritva Saarikko photo from the *Before And after Science* sessions.

Left: Two of Peter Schmidt's prints that came free with the first UK pressing only of Before and After Science. These are now very collectable.

Low, Heroes, Before And After Science and Cluster & Eno 1977

1977 was the year the music press was calling 'year zero'. Punk rock had become the music of choice for reviewers and writers and that also bled through to record executives who scoured every pub in the land to sign up any band who was playing three chords and being spat at. Suddenly all the music and bands of the last ten years were dismissed as dinosaurs or boring old farts. 'Never trust a hippie' was a slogan and the press set out to bury bands like ELP and Yes and anything that smacked of instrumental virtuosity. Oddly both Bowie and Eno escaped the wrath of both the punks and the vitriolic music press. Many of the punks who formed bands were actually Bowie and Roxy fans (there are even some photos of Sid Vicious in a Bowie T-shirt). Siouxsie and the Bromley contingent were seen at the most recent concerts by both Bowie and Roxy Music.

Both Eno and Bowie were interested in punk as a passing phenomenon (Bowie even requesting albums by The Stranglers etc. to listen to), but in the world, both artists were creating for themselves and far away from the British music press, they seemed almost blissfully unaware of the seismic shift that was happening in the UK where their new music was at odds with both current and old trends. It was two years later that the work that they were producing would be co-opted by the next musical trend/fashion that would declare both Bowie and Roxy as being its initial flame and torch bearers.

At the end of 1976, Bowie had presented his new album to his record company and they were not best pleased. Not only did most of the songs have an odd angular quality to them but there was a whole side where the golden larynx of Bowie was completely missing. They were not sure what to do with it and the only song they saw as a possibility was 'Sound And Vision' and even then, Bowie's voice didn't hit in until the halfway point. Bowie had relocated to Hansa Studios in Berlin in October to finish the album with mixing and overdubs so that it now sounded different than the version of songs recorded in Paris. He gave RCA the tapes in early November and they sat on releasing the album until after the Christmas period thinking that the record would bomb, so they buried it in the January releases and did little promotion of the record either. When it was finally released, it reached number two in the UK album charts and number 11 in the US *Billboard* charts. Seeing they had a hit album, RCA eventually released 'Sound And Vision' as a 7" single in January, where it reached number three in the UK singles charts, and it would be Bowie's last Top 10 single of the seventies.

David Bowie: Low (1977)

Personnel:
David Bowie: vocals, guitar, piano, harmonica
Brian Eno: synthesizer
George Murray: bass
Dennis Davis: percussion
Roy Young: piano
Carlos Alomar: rhythm guitar
All songs by David Bowie unless stated
Recorded at: Le Château d'Hérouville and Hansa Tonstudio
Released: 14 January 1977
Record Label: RCA
Highest Chart Position: UK: 2; US: 11
Tracklisting: Side One: 1. Speed Of Life, 2. Breaking Glass (Bowie, Davis, Murray), 3. What In The World, 4. Sound And Vision, 5. Always Crashing In The Same Car, 6. Be My Wife, 7. A New Career In A New Town. Side Two: 1. Warszawa (Eno, Bowie), 2. Art Decade, 3. Weeping Wall, 4. Subterraneans

It is hard to discuss a track-by-track breakdown of *Low* in relation to Eno because we can only trace one track that we know he had a greater input in (this would change when they recorded *Heroes*). 'Warszawa''s chiming bass note hangs ominously in the air as the Chamberlin adds chord flourishes over the top; its main melody is melancholic and uses minor keys. It's quite odd because it sounds unlike any other Eno composition of the time and it feels dramatic but somehow downbeat at the same time. The use of synthesizers seems to give a semblance of a place and time and oddly, some people have referred to it as a Weimar-era-inspired piece. 'Warszawa''s main theme is one of disquiet, something that Eno would follow through on an instrumental piece on the next Bowie album.

We know Eno is present on the song 'Sound And Vision' as we can clearly hear him doing the 'doo doo' backing vocals along with Tony Visconti's then-wife Mary Hopkin. The other track we can clearly hear his presence is on 'Art Decade' with its drum machine rhythm pattern and its scattering synth sound, and this was one of the tracks that the instrumentation was filled out in Bowie's absence. Its melody is majestic and simple-sounding but has enough going on to create an atmosphere all of its own; it's not exactly gallery music but has certainly been used on some art documentaries in the last 45 years.

Even though Eno is only credited as co-songwriter on one of the tracks on *Low,* he can be heard as a big influence on many of the pieces on the album, especially its second side and is commonly cited as the inspiration for Bowie's new direction. The critics at the time were firmly split in two, some admiring Bowie for his daring experimentation and new direction while others felt he was shooting his own stellar career dead. Since its release, *Low* has often been critically reported to be Bowie's best album or at least within the top three albums he ever produced. Sheppard quotes an interview with Eno by Stephen Dalton about the album:

Although I had quite a lot to do with Low, it was definitely, at source, his (Bowie's) record. I wasn't even there from the start. I think my contribution gave it a different shading that it wouldn't have had otherwise because I was pushing for all the strange instrumental stuff and for the sound to be radical in some way, all nervy and electronic …

In the end, *Low* helped change public perception of Bowie and made him into an art music icon, allowing him to finally shake off the Ziggy Stardust image of old. It also meant that Bowie would want to repeat the experiment again a few months later, with Eno realising that he could still continue a successful career whilst also moving on to a new musical path. Bowie's hunch had paid off and it was thanks to his association with Eno that he had managed to steer his career into fresh waters and away from the derision meted out to most of the other rock stars of the early seventies. For Eno, though, he then had the problem of working on his next solo album to contend with as it had been up to two years since his last album, so anything else was a distraction, but strangely these distractions also influenced his next phase of songwriting.

Eno had already been working on some new material at Basing Street Studios for the last year, but he felt that none of it had any merit and even the use of the Oblique Strategies wasn't solving the sense of inertia that he was feeling with the whole exercise and in fact, the sessions had come to a standstill. In *Sounds* paper in February of 1977, when Eno's stock was at its highest, he comes across as almost morose at the lack of momentum for his own album. He was apparently unrecognisable from the strutting peacock of 1973 as he quietly discussed how he was slowly becoming a hermit in his own home with only Ritva Saarikko for company. In an article for the *Melody Maker* the same week as the *Sounds* article, Eno wrote a diary of his week which began with the confession, 'I have been trying to write some music, with little success. All I can think about is how much I'd like to be sitting alone in a cinema.'

Eno pulled in his usual retinue of musicians to help him get over his writer's block. These included Manzanera, Fripp, Phil Collins, Paul Rudolph, Brian Turrington, Bill MacCormick, Percy Jones, and a member of Krautrock band Can, the drummer Jaki Liebezeit. Eno himself also took on more instrumental duties than ever before on a record. It was around this time that Eno also got dragged along to see the band Talking Heads' first London show, and he was impressed by what he heard and afterwards got introduced to the band backstage. After a discussion with singer David Byrne, it was agreed that Eno would produce the next album by the band. But first, he had not only his album to work on, but he was also about to leave for Berlin to start work on Bowie's follow-up album to *Low* and hopefully record some more pieces with Roedelius and Moebius for a possible album that would be released in Germany only.

Before going to the Hansa studio in Berlin, Eno spent June at Conny Plank's studio in Cologne with Cluster, recording a series of tracks that were eventually released later in the year as *Cluster & Eno* on Sky Records. These recordings were mainly of an ambient nature and Asmus Tietchens, on his sleeve notes for the 2009 reissue of the album, states that the album 'might even lay claim to be the first-ever ambient production on German soil'.

The three musicians worked closely together, starting where they had left off the previous year. There were no Oblique Strategies and no concept or a particular type of working style to be forced on to the recording made. Sheppard quotes Eno on the making of the album:

It nearly always started out like people would jam today against a sequencer, though we weren't using sequencers then; somebody would become sort of a human sequencer – maybe Roedelius repeating a pattern on the keyboard … My problem with jamming with people before was that they would always change too quickly and they'd never listen to where they were. With Cluster, we could stay in the same place for 25 minutes or so, really get into the details of a piece, start to feel it as a landscape, not as just a moment in the music, but as a place.

Plank and Eno worked together sculpturing the sound of the recordings as sessions progressed and even Can's bassist Holger Czukay popped into the studio to cover a few licks to the track 'Ho Renomo'. The finished album was a mixture of melancholic piano études mixed with vibrant synth sounds and treated guitars, and one track even had the extra sonic and exotic instrumentation of an Indian tambura that added a drone sound beneath the song 'One'. The album was finally released in August and would be seen as a stopgap recording before Eno's next solo album, which finally came out in December.

Cluster & Eno: Cluster & Eno (1977)

Personnel:
Brian Eno
Dieter Moebius
Hans-Joachim Roedelius
All songs written by Cluster & Eno
Produced by: Conny Plank
Recorded at: Conny Plank Studio, Cologne, Germany
Released by: Sky Records
Highest Chart Position: –
Tracklisting: Side One: 1. Ho Renomo, 2. Schöne Hände, 3. Steinsame, 4. Wehrmut. Side Two: 1. Mit Simaen. 2. Selange, 3. Die Bunge, 4. One, 5. Für Luise

'Ho Renomo' starts as contemplative arpeggiating piano chords over which electronics drone and hum and Czukay's bass gives a bottom-end clang to the airy synthesizer patterns over the top. The chord sequences move at a meditative pace and the piece almost hangs frozen in the air. Again, I must point out it's hard to tell exactly what Eno is playing on any of these tracks as there is no information about individual instruments from the performers apart from the guest musicians.

'Schöne Hände' has electronics that hover like flies as deep bass synth notes rumble beneath; these could be attributed to Eno because they have a similar structure to what would appear on *Before And After Science* later in the year. Orchestral and string pads repeat in a cyclical manner for 'Steinsame' and the sound seems to take its cues from 'Warszawa' in having a slightly melancholic feel to it, plus the sound of the instrumentation creates a similar atmosphere over its repeating chord structure. 'Wehrmut' uses synths to create a set of uneasy but drifting sounds as it moves slowly through its own landscape. One synth plays the closest thing to a melody over the top at the higher end of the scale, but the music's overall feel is that with a connection between landscape and memory. This also feels like a piece that would inform some of the newer sections added to *Music For Films* when it gets rereleased in 1978.

'Mit Simaen' is a short piano piece swathed in reverb and echo, so it sounds like it is being played in a vast cathedral and shares many elements to Harold Budd's sound a year later; here, it sounds like Eno is more evident on the production side. Jaunty jazz piano chords and an odd drum pattern are the template for 'Selange', its other piano notes falling like rain over the top of this chord sequence. 'Die Bunge' has electronic squeaks and the kind of space that you would find in a Stockhausen piece. This then gives way to some humming bass notes that fill out the sound and then a slight lite melody.

'One' has the Indian drone that carries the piece through and somehow feels a little out of place on this album as it drags it slightly into the world music category, which it most definitely isn't. The other sounds atonally berate the traditional instrumentation making it the most avant-garde and noisiest piece on the entire album. It seems like a strange decision to use an instrument mainly associated with psychedelia in the recent history of rock music and it makes the piece seem somehow disconnected from the electronic and piano-based études that make up the rest of the album. 'Für Luise' points the way ahead in sound for Eno, one that he would embrace more in the eighties. A series of Satie-like piano notes play over synth pads which gives a sedate sound.

Like its follow-up in 1978, the *Cluster & Eno* album was only available in the UK via import which made it quite a costly item in 1977 especially since some shops had to specially import it. It finally got a rerelease in 2009, when the internet became the great leveller for getting hold of import albums. These are important releases for Eno as you begin to hear him steer his ship towards a more Germanic Krautrock-influenced sound on his next solo release.

However, before Eno could get back to Basing Street Studios to resume work on his album, he first had to fly to Berlin to meet up with Bowie to start work on the follow-up to *Low* and he arrived there in early July. Rather than working on the album in two studios, Bowie had opted to work at Hansa Studios which sat right next to the Berlin Wall near what was the pre-war Potsdamer Platz that was (and now is again) a large public square at the centre of Berlin. But at the time when *Heroes* was recorded, the square had been cut in half by the wall and many of the buildings close to it were in a slightly dilapidated state, including the Hansa studio. The studio itself had a large control room on another floor with cables that had to run from the large ballroom recording studio beneath where Bowie, Eno and Visconti would utilise the room's natural ambience. Apparently, the studio had been used to host parties during the Nazi era, and now Russian troops could gaze into the window of the control booth from their posts on the wall and watch the musicians working, and being so close they could probably hear some of the music being created there.

Berlin was the city where both Bowie and Iggy Pop then spent most of their time, living in a flat found for them by Tangerine Dream's Edgar Froese and spending their time being anonymous in the city. Bowie painted expressionist-style paintings and he and Iggy went to the local bars and drank beer of an evening. Tobias Ruther, in his 2014 book *Heroes: David Bowie And Berlin,* makes an observation about the three albums now lumbered under the title of the 'Berlin Trilogy' and how the city is represented on them:

There are 32 tracks in what is called the Berlin Triptych. The name of the city isn't mentioned in a single one of them. If Bowie does ever refer to parts of the city of Berlin, he misspells them. And he does this not just once, but twice even (reminding one of Kunze talking of how the word 'inept' never normally applied to Bowie). The first time this happens is in 'Neuköln' (instead of 'Neukölln'), the next to last instrumental on 'Heroes', which, with its atonal, orientalising saxophone, gives most the impression of documentary truth on the album.

Even though what Ruther says is true, we cannot ignore the overriding influence of this city cut off from the rest of western Europe on both Bowie and Eno and especially on the ambience that overrides many of the tracks on *Heroes*.

Eno did, of course, bring along his Oblique Strategies to use for alternative ways of working on tracks during the recording, a strict adherence to what the cards would say would be observed; these had the biggest influence on side two of the album as Thomas Jerome Seabrook in his 2008 book *Bowie In Berlin* discusses:

Bowie and Eno imposed various rules and constraints on the recording process that helped lend the material a tension to match the songs

71

on side one. Their musical path would often be led by Eno's Oblique Strategies cards, which frequently took both off in unexpected directions. Sometimes this meant leaving the outcome entirely to chance. The most tangible example of this is when each would record a track (or several) on his own and then, before the other added his, push down the sliders, leaving them both unsure as to exactly what they were working with. Then at a predetermined end-point, they would bring up the faders and listen, for the first time, to what they had produced.

This chance element between the pair made Eno consider the *Heroes* album as a far more collaborative record than *Low* and Eno received more co-writing credits on this album than on the previous one. According to Eno, the only song that was written by Bowie before the recording process started was 'Sons Of The Silent Age', an almost typical sounding Bowie work in its structure. Bowie began to work getting backing tracks down at his usual breakneck speed, making Eno's more methodical approach seem tortoise-like in comparison. Sheppard quotes an interview with Eno about the early stages of the album:

It was much harder working on 'Heroes' than 'Low', Eno later admitted. The whole thing, except 'Sons Of The Silent Age', which was written beforehand, was evolved on the spot in the studio. Not only that, everything on the album is a first take! I mean, we did second takes, but they weren't as good. It was all done in a very casual kind of way.

This randomness mainly worked in Eno's favour, especially because if songs were taking longer to put together, Bowie became detached or distracted during the recording process, leaving most of the work for Eno to painstakingly add to and put together. Obviously, not all the experiments in sound worked and a percentage ended up never being used for the album, but this process did help any impasses that the duo sometimes hit on long days in the studio.

Again, Bowie called on Murray, Davis and Alomar to lay down their basic tracks, which Eno and Bowie transformed into fully-fledged songs. The only other musician to join them was Robert Fripp, who was especially flown in to add some lead guitar to mainly the title track. He was invited over after being called on the phone by Eno, who thought that the song 'Heroes' needed some Fripp on it. It's generally accepted 'Bowie lore' that Fripp was only in Berlin for 48 hours, going straight from the airport to the studio with his guitar and being told by Eno to set up immediately. Fripp says that most of his guitar parts, including his incredible guitar line on the title track, were done in just one take, with Fripp working quickly so he could visit some Berlin 'establishments' before catching his flight home. How true this all is, is hard to tell, but there appears to be plenty of posed-for photos of the three men in the studio during his brief visit. Fripp's studio session lasted over six hours, with Eno processing his guitar through his trusty VCS3 in the same way the pair created *(No Pussyfooting)*, and the first piece Fripp worked on was 'Beauty And The Beast'. Nearly all of his first-take performances both Eno and Bowie thought were perfect.

During the recording sessions, there was much humour and laughing involved, with both Bowie and Eno adopting the guise of comedians Peter Cook and Dudley Moore's characters 'Derek and Clive' who had recently released some risqué albums full of expletives on Island Records. This jocularity seems quite at odds with the moribund music that was being produced for the album. The album was a critical and commercial success when it was released, reaching number three in the UK charts but did less well in the US, only managing number 35, becoming Bowie's worst-selling album there since *Hunky Dory*. Two singles were released from the album – 'Heroes' and 'Beauty And The Beast' – and both failed to get into the Top 20 UK singles charts.

David Bowie: Heroes (1977)

Personnel:
David Bowie: vocals, keyboards, guitar, saxophone, koto
Brian Eno: synthesizer, keyboards, effects (guitar treatments)
George Murray: bass
Robert Fripp: lead guitar
Dennis Davis: percussion
Carlos Alomar: rhythm guitar
All songs written by David Bowie unless stated
Produced by: Tony Visconti and David Bowie
Recorded at: Hansa Tonstudio
Released: 14 October 1977
Record Label: RCA Victor
Highest Chart Position: UK: 3; US: 35
Tracklisting: Side One: 1. Beauty And The Beast, 2. Joe The Lion, 3. Heroes (Bowie, Eno), 4. Sons Of The Silent Age, 5. Blackout. Side Two: 1. V-2

Schneider, 2. Sense Of Doubt, 3. Moss Garden (Bowie, Eno), 4. Neuköln (Bowie, Eno), 5. The Secret Life Of Arabia (Bowie, Eno, Alomar)

'Beauty And The Beast' is a harsh opening to the album, more so than 'Speed Of Life' on *Low*. This is a jerky, almost one-chord song that belies its funk rhythm by adding crackling two-note keyboard parts and an atonal lead from Fripp (actually, Fripp had recoded at least four lead guitar parts for this song, and all were used with some manipulation from Eno). Bowie's lyrics are impressionistic and obscure, sounding more like tone poems, but the duality of self-reference some have seen as Bowie burying his 'Thin White Duke' character ready to now embrace his 'artist in Berlin' character; this has also been put down to his love-hate relationship with drugs and the slow process of weaning himself off cocaine. The song also became one of the harshest 7" single releases of 1977, which is saying quite a lot as it reached number 38 in the UK charts and became Bowie's worst-selling single in five years.

'Joe The Lion' appears to almost take off from where the barrage of 'Beauty And The Beast' leaves off. Again, Fripp's guitar tumbles over itself, apparently created under instruction from Bowie to play like blues guitarist Albert King. Bowie's vocals travel its widest range during the song, with its lyrics allegedly about his son Zowie (now called Duncan); as appeared in some reviews at the time, it has been later claimed that they are about avant-garde artist Chris Burdon who was famous for nailing himself to the bonnet of a Volkswagen car. Apparently, Bowie improvised and free-formed the lyrics in less than an hour. Eno's keyboards can be heard most prominently during the song's quiet section where Bowie announces, 'It's Monday.' The song musically seems to be a nod towards Krautrock giants Faust who had scored a hit album in the UK with *The Faust Tapes* purely because it was sold at the same price as a 7" single.

To be honest, the title song of the album, 'Heroes', is almost worth a small chapter, especially as its stature has grown so considerably over the years. It is also Eno's first co-writing credit on the album and the song that most people probably associate with him outside his fan base. It's almost hard to believe now that when the track was released as a single, it only scraped as high as number 24 in the UK charts. After the angular guitar of the first two tracks, Fripp's fretwork is majestic and monumental as the track opens, and its walking bass line and major scale piano chords all begin to build as the track progresses. Eno had spent almost a week shaping the sound, wanting something that gave a similar ambience to music created by Krautrock bands such as Can. Once the basic tracks had been laid down by Bowie, Alomar, Murray and Davis, sounds began to be altered by Eno, giving the track more and more bottom end as it progressed so that it sounds like the piece slowly swelling as it goes along. Fripp's guitar was then added with Eno manipulating it in real-time and then making minor adjustments after the guitarist had left. Bowie then added some brass parts and then extra percussion was used; the track was left as an instrumental and Bowie wanted it that way until the 11th hour when he decided to add some vocals.

Bowie's lyric for the track has come under a lot of discussion over the years, but it is generally understood that it starts off as being influenced by a painting in the Brücke Museum of German expressionist art called 'Lovers Between Garden Walls' by Otto Mueller. The other would be the now-famous incident that he witnessed from the control room at the Hansa studios of Visconti (who was at the time married to Mary Hopkin) having an illicit embrace in the shadow of the wall with Antonia Maass (who would add some backing vocals to the album). Bowie moments later delivered the most impassioned, and some say finest, vocal of his career when his producer re-entered the studio.

'Sons Of The Silent Age' is an effortless late seventies Bowie song that has more to do with his incredible songwriting technique than it does with any trickery that Eno could have added to the piece. Its words conjure images of intellectuals in Weimar Berlin and with its soaring sax and vocal lines, conjures up images of that era. Side one ends with 'Blackout', a foot-stomping rocker that has Eno's chirping synthesizer battling it out with Fripp's slightly atonal lead. Eno's sound manipulation is rife on the song and Bowie's lyrics are some of his bleakest as he discusses blacking out after too much drinking, something that had happened to him fairly recently.

Like *Low*, it's on side two where we see Eno's biggest influence on the album and the fact that he gets a writing credit for three of the five tracks speaks volumes. 'V-2 Schneider' is a paean to Kraftwerk's Florian Schneider and to the V-2 rocket that did so much damage to the UK during the Second World War; strangely, Schneider never commented about the song, although Kraftwerk themselves had name-checked Bowie on their song 'Trans Europe Express'. Eno's phased synth fade in the track before the piece becomes slightly more urgent while Eno throws as many sounds at the song as he can muster, taking what would be a basic rolling rock plodder into more avant-garde and Krautrock territory.

'Sense Of Doubt' is one of the bleakest instrumentals Bowie ever created, its downward spiralling four-note piano riff hangs like a heavy cloud in the air and is the coldest piece Bowie would execute on vinyl. Bowie and Eno had consulted the Oblique Strategies during the compositional process and Eno's card had read 'Try to make everything as similar as possible' whilst Bowie's had read 'Emphasise differences'. Neither knew what the other's card had said, and they both worked on the piece without revealing to the other what their instruction was. It's strange here that Eno doesn't get a co-writing credit when obviously half the track is created by him.

Synthesized crashes lead from the previous track into the co-written 'Moss Garden'. For this track, Bowie wanted to create a meditative, stately piece of music based on an actual moss garden that Bowie had visited in Kyoto in Japan. Eno laid down many layers of slow, undulating synthesizer chords over which Bowie plucked at his koto, a Japanese traditional instrument, letting some notes hang in the air while others would come across as being busy. The track almost feels like a sense of relief after some of the pieces that have preceded it and the piece almost meanders along. 'Neuköln', a track about one of the poorest areas of Berlin (although spelt incorrectly), is a mournful piece of music with Eno adding musique concrète sounds beneath Bowie's squealing sax playing giving the whole piece a sense of unease. Again, Eno builds up a barrage of synthetic sounds, which are hard to place what they are trying to sound like. The track's atmosphere is dour and the last few notes are screeched out into the silence on Bowie's sax. The album ends with 'The Secret Life Of Arabia', an almost jaunty song to close the album, which hangs its chordal structure on a mainly Eastern scale. Eno provides some of his most rock-style playing since *Taking Tiger Mountain* and Bowie tries to funk up proceedings on the piano. The lyrics and music begin to self-reference Bowie's other songs, with 'Speed Of Life' etc. being mentioned. The track's uptempo beat and music feels like a severe jump cut musically on what has happened before and feels somewhat out of place on the album, although it would hint at the musical style that Bowie and Eno would adopt for his next record in 1979.

An instrumental outtake by Eno and Bowie was released on the Rykodisc 1991 reissue of the album titled 'Abdulmajid', and seems to have been recorded during these sessions as it sounds similar to the other instrumentals on the album in its overall feel. The track hints more at the Krautrock end with its drum machine drenched in reverb and echo while

Eno and Bowie layer synth sounds over the top; it probably would have fitted well on the second side of the album and maybe would have made a better closing track to it.

In a 1978 interview with Bowie for the *Melody Maker Book Of Bowie* magazine with Michael Watts, Bowie discusses his working relationship with Eno:

> What has he injected into my music? Is probably the more accurate question, and what he's injected is a totally new way of looking at it, or another reason for writing. He got me off narration, which I was so intolerably bored with. Brian really opened my eyes to the idea of processing, to the abstract of communication. I don't think we agree with each other on everything. We're certainly not that simpatico where we embrace what each other says with open arms.

This time RCA decided to go on a promotional overdrive for the album after pretty much ignoring *Low*, double-page spreads in the music press claiming, 'There's Old Wave, there's New Wave and there's David Bowie'. Eno returned to London once the recording was finished and hopefully started work on his now abandoned fourth solo album; working with both Cluster and Bowie had been a welcome distraction from the headache that his own record had become. Also, whilst back in London, he oversaw the final batch of recordings for his Obscure label that actually wouldn't see the light of day until the following year.

Eno was getting stressed about the new album and suffering from bouts of insomnia as he pulled musicians into Basing Street Studios to improvise pieces that he instructed them to do off the top of his head while he played around with some heavy dub-style reverb. In the end, Eno almost cut his losses and chose versions of pieces already worked on, played with them and cobbled them together to make a final album. Eno called the album *Before And After Science* in a tribute to the way he selected tracks to further work on from the vast array of recordings made so far. Sheppard interviews guitarist Fred Frith about Eno's attitude while making the album:

> I think the album was trying for him because his heart wasn't in it. He was in the process of intellectually formulating a completely different way of thinking about music, and in a way, what we were doing was too much like his older way of doing things. So he had to shed it. We didn't know it at the time, but it became obvious in retrospect.

DECADES | Brian Eno in the 70s

Apart from the musical aspect, another idea and problem was going around Eno's head – the blending of contemporary modern artists with the music being created. In a strange way, this was about the mass production and mechanisation of modern art to open it up to a wider audience. Eno discussed this idea with Peter Schmidt and tried to figure out a way he could incorporate this into his next album release. This would, in effect, mean persuading his record company to pay for the mass production of a series of quality prints that would be an intrinsic part of the music on the album and its overall package. Eno wanted to bring the art gallery into people's living rooms and create a kind of mini installation with the music into the homes of purchasers. In the end, only a limited quantity of Schmidt's paintings as prints were available on the first pressing of Eno's album (and are now very hard to find) and the idea would be either eventually dropped or nixed by the record company for any future album releases. Even those who bought later copies of *Before And After Science* had to put up with tiny reproductions of Schmidt's work on the back of the album sleeve. Even though Eno was thinking of these things as a distraction from his album, he felt that it might also enhance the music that he felt was below par but actually turned out to be one of his most acclaimed recordings; this was also Eno's last solo foray into rock music in the seventies.

Brian Eno: Before And After Science (1977)

Personnel:
Brian Eno: vocals, guitar, piano, synthesizer (AKS, CS-80, Moog), vibraphone, bells
Phil Collins: drums and percussion
Percy Jones: bass
Paul Rudolph: bass
Brian Turrington: bass
Bill MacCormick: bass
Fred Frith: guitar
Mobi Moebius: piano
Achim Roedelius: piano
Dave Mattacks: drums
Phil Manzanera: guitar
Jaki Liebezeit: drums
All songs written by Brian Eno
Produced by: Brian Eno and Rhett Davies

Recorded at: Basing Street Studios, London
Released: December 1977
Highest Chart Position: –
Tracklisting: Side One: 1. No One Receiving, 2. Backwater, 3. Kurt's Rejoinder,
4. Energy Fools The Magician, 5. King's Lead Hat. Side Two: 1. Here he
Comes, 2. Julie With…, 3. By This River, 4. Through Hollow Lands (For
Harold Budd), 5. Spider And I

It had taken Eno almost two years to record the album, stopping and
starting around other projects that he was asked to do. In the end, he
had recorded around 100 pieces of music for the album, but unlike the
tracks for *Another Green World,* the vast majority of these would not be
reused in a different form or even released. Eno had referred to *Another
Green World* as 'sky music' and talked about *Before And After Science*
as 'ocean music'; this is pretty self-explanatory when you read the lyrics
to the album as there are a considerable amount of water references on
it. Unlike *Another Green World,* that had its small vignette-style tracks
that break up the main narrative of the album, Eno eschewed this kind
of track listing to make the record have songs that break the two-minute
mould. He also took a leaf out of Bowie's book by placing the quieter
material on side two and the more energetic workouts on the first side.
The sound of the album certainly doesn't hint at its protracted and
troubled gestation, in fact, the pieces are the most streamlined in sound
that Eno had produced to date. As always, Eno's lyrics for the album are
fairly ambiguous and any reading of them as a straight narrative is hard
to do, although some pieces can be discussed within an alleged narrative
framework. The author Simon Reynolds once described the songs as
having themes of 'boredom' and 'bliss'.

In an interview with Tom Carson in the *Enovations* magazine dated
summer 1979, Eno discusses his lyric writing for *Before And After Science*:

When I talk about the way I write my lyrics, I always talk about the part
of the lyric-writing that I think is unique. I don't talk about the bit where
I write lyrics like everyone else – I assume people don't want to know
about that. It does lay rather too much stress on a technique, which is
nonetheless the central technique, but not the only technique. First of all,
songs start in different ways. Sometimes – though quite rarely – there will
be a literary idea at the beginning of something before there's any music.
They nearly all start out as instrumentals, really. The ones that don't start

out with an explicit idea usually start off with the idea that they're going to be instrumentals. And at some point, I think this is going to end up as a song, and so then I do the mix of the piece – in a fairly expanded form, with most instruments on that are going to be there in the end. I take it home and just start singing over it, and I do this by playing it very loud, and just singing all the time, just running it back and singing again … I record everything I do, and then I just sit and listen to it all.

Eno appears then to have cherry-picked lines from these improvised vocal performances and puts them together to make the lyrics for the song, giving an air of almost William Burroughs cut-up-like randomness to them.

'No One Receiving' starts off with Rudolph, Collins and Jones doing their best approximation of a dub sound, with Eno's guitar giving the track a little Nile Rogers Chic-style funk to the piece. Synthesizers buzz-saw away, making sure the piece is firmly kept in an avant-garde style mode with Collins's percussion rolling around over the top of it. According to Russell Mills in the book *More Dark Than Shark*, the line 'On its metalled ways' is taken from T S Eliot's 'Burnt Norton'. Eric Tamm breaks down Eno's vocal songs into categories and claims that 'No One Receiving' is an 'assaultive' song because they have atonal elements and 'crash against and wear away the shore of the musically acceptable'. I'm not sure this can be attributed to this song as Eno's vocals certainly carry a strong melody to them throughout.

'Backwater' is certainly the most pop-like song on the album and probably would have made a good single release from it. The song appears to be about a group of six people, including the 'porter's'daughters', almost set adrift at sea. Some have read the lyrics as being about cannibalism because of the line 'There were six of us, but now we are five', but this could also be a slice of Eno nonsense just added because it rhymed or fitted in with the rhythm of this rather jaunty, piano-driven number. As Eno points out in the Tom Carson interview:

I find that I've actually got a whole section of verbiage to go through, and then I make a big chart up, quite often, and I write down all the lines in their relevant places on the verse.

Funkier rhythms abound on 'Kurt's Rejoinder' although many feel the track has a more jazz flavour with Dave Mattacks' shuffling drum pattern that runs throughout, but here again, it's Jones' tumbling bass that really adds something to the song, as it manages to be both jazzy and funky at the same time. It also features a sample of the voice of German artist Kurt Schwitters from his 1930 recording of 'Sonate In Urlauten' (called 'Ur Sonata' on the album), a Dadaist poem that he performed at the time. The use of this would also hint at a direction that Eno began to take in the early 1980s. Eno said of this track that it was 'an experiment in how to have voices without the focus of the singer'.

'Energy Fools The Magician' (a title that some thought referenced a tarot card reading) is a jazz-sounding piece with Collins using mainly cymbals and Jones being almost mercurial on his dexterous bass playing over the top. It's only Eno's morose-sounding synthesizer chords over the top that ground the track in any way. Fred Frith's modified guitar wails away in the background like the call of a siren beneath the scattershot percussion and stately synth sounds.

'King's Lead Hat', an anagram of the name of the band 'Talking Heads', finishes side one, and this was released as a single in January 1978. This can be seen as Eno taking on the influence, or at least recognising, the sound of new wave bands at the time with its clipped vocals that bark out their words. The odd thing here is that songs like 'Third Uncle' were proto-punk songs two years before punk even existed, so is this Eno paying homage to the new wave or being self-referential and saying, 'I did this first and can still do it'? Eno's vocals take on a David Byrne-like delivery while Manzanera shreds his guitar chords and Fripp's lead is one of his most restrained performances of the seventies. The song charges ahead at full pace and Eno's lyrics have an almost Edward Lear-esque nonsense value to them as he proclaims, 'The passage of my life is measured out in shirts.'

Side two of the album is where the more sedate songs rest and is probably the more fulfilling side to repeat listen to, its languid mood giving the listener a mental space for contemplation as the songs slowly drift by you. It is this side that features most of Eno's 'water lyrics' and these suit the mood better than the over-ambitious word count of some of the tracks on side one.

It starts off with the almost country music-style guitar stylings of 'Here He Comes', a song that it is often seen as an outsider lyric where Eno intones 'The boy who tried to vanish to another time, is no longer here with his sad blue eyes'. This seems to hint at someone who is displaced and maybe searching for a 'golden age', a return to a point in time they think is better than now, and this oddly was a theme that Bowie also covered as well. Eric Tamm in *The Vertical Colour of Sound* discusses the song:

[Whether] 'Here He Comes' must be judged too long depends on the receptivity of the listener and the mode of listening. In the linear, horizontal mode, little or nothing seems to 'happen' for the piece's duration; but listened to vertically, the song reveals a perpetual play of timbral and motivic elements: strip away the drums, voice, and steady pulse, and we are not far from the ambient style.

Manzanera's guitar work is outstanding beneath Eno's sad lyric, and his piano playing is some of Eno's best work on the instrument; it's also a good introductory mood for the rest of the album as it moves into a more contemplative mode.

'Julie With…' is one of the water songs that has a sense of calm and innocence which starts to become threatened as the song takes a strange dark turn. Eno sings, 'The still sea is darker than before' and suddenly, the track takes on an ominous feeling that changes the whole mood of the piece away from it being romantic to something sinister. One American writer claimed that the song was about Eno wanting to sexually assault the character 'Julie' when their boat is far enough out at sea, although another commentator thought that he murdered her. Some believe it was about the actress Julie Christie after Eno was spied sharing a taxicab with her in New York, but whatever it's about, the track is not quite as languid as it first sets out to be.

'By This River' is a piece written with Roedelius and Moebius, which we can kind of assume, came from recordings that the trio made during the summer rather than at the recordings made the year before. Its Satie-like piano chords are infused with a baroque beauty, while over the top Eno delivers a slight but wistful CS-80 solo and subdued lyric. The words seemed to be about another romantic interlude, but this time one where the couple are slowly becoming distant from each other. It's not quite clear how Eno managed to lift this track away from what would be the trio's next album for his sole use on his own solo album, the song, though, fits perfectly the atmosphere Eno is trying to create with this side of the album.

'Through Hollow Lands' is dedicated to Harold Budd, whom Eno worked with during the summer for his Obscure release. It has never been explained why he would dedicate the piece to him, but this surely must have impressed Budd enough to create two albums with him in later. The piece chimes with bell-like synthesizers and Fred Frith's cascading guitar notes, MacCormick's bass is steady and unfussy, and the mood certainly references Budd's work. It is also placed within exactly the same part of the track listing that the other instrumental piece of the album is on side one, almost as if they were mirroring each other in some way, like yin and yang.

The album closes with 'Spider And I', a majestic song that Eno plays all the instruments on except for the bass. Again, the lyrics seem to hint at being separated from the real world as if someone is gazing out of a window and watching events go by: 'Spider and I sit watching the sky, On a world without sound'. It's as if the narrator is taking time out to dream awhile as the skyscape floats by; the fact that he dreams of a 'ship that sails away' also gives the song a sense of longing.

The album would be placed at number 14 in the *NME*'s end-of-year chart that rounded up the year's releases in order of greatness, faring better than certain punk and new wave records at the time. The fact that Bowie's *Heroes* topped the chart meant that Eno was certainly not out of touch or a dinosaur in music's year zero.

As mentioned, initial copies of the album came with four prints by Peter Schmidt entitled: 'The Road To The Crater', 'Look At September, Look At October', 'The Other House' and 'Four Years'. The original album cover was also painted by Schmidt, showing Eno reflected in a mirror sitting at a table that has dice, paints and brushes, Oblique Strategies and a cat, while in the background can be seen Eno's beloved reel-to-reel tape recorders. In the end the cover used was a black-and-white close-up photo of Eno's face taken by Ritva Saarikko and Eno fans would have to wait until the summer of 1979 to see an original Schmidt painting reproduced on the cover of the 'Enovations' newsletter.

1977 had been a busy and very visual year for Eno and he managed to sidestep the fallout from punk, and he had been part of the creation of what would become known as three of the classic albums released that year. He had been in demand as a producer and had written and co-written many pieces of new work. But for some reason, there was a darkness hanging over him as the yuletide period came around. Eno had begun to question his very method of working and wondering where next he should go musically in the future. Eno discusses some of his problems in an interview with Ian MacDonald of the *NME* published on 3 December 1977:

I abandoned the album three times before I finished it. It really caused a lot of sweat and heartache. At one point, I thought I could never achieve anything more, musically. Not that I'd achieved everything, just that there was nowhere else for me to go. It affected everything I did in the end. I found myself saying, 'You're just a dilettante. You're not doing anything with the kind of intensity that it deserves.' It was a crisis of confidence that went very deep.

I use the word 'science' to indicate techniques and rational knowledge. And what the title implies is that the condition 'before science' is similar to the condition 'after' it – that there's a kind of circle thing and that science is the isolated one. I used to be led by the work. Something would happen and I'd just follow it. This time it wasn't as easy as that. Things seemed to be going in directions which weren't interesting to me anymore – I found myself trying to use a technique which was bound to give a particular class of outputs to give a different class. So, I was working against the technique, to some extent. I suspect that I've come to the end of a way of working with this record. It's a loss of confidence and I think that comes through – something more like humanity than whimsicality. Not so much tentativeness as reasonable doubt.

This sense of doubt in his own work tied in with the fact that Eno would almost disappear off the radar in the UK as a performer and recording artist.

The Year Of Distraction: 'After The Heat' 1978

Actually, Eno's quiet year started off with a bit of a bang as his record company decided to release 'King's Lead Hat' as a 7" single in January. The record did not make a dent in the UK charts but has since become one of Eno's most sought-after items because of its B side. This is a song co-written by Eno and the band Snatch, who were in fact, Eno's old friend Judy Nylon and the musician Patti Palladin. The track is called 'R.A.F.' and rather than a piece about Britain's flying corps it was actually about Germany's 'Red Army Faction', also known as the 'Baader-Meinhof Group', a group who committed random acts of terrorism with a militant far-left agenda during the early part of the seventies, however, their activities would peak during 1977 which led to a national crisis called the 'German Autumn'. In total, the group have been held responsible for 34 deaths, including heads of banks and industrialists. For someone who had refused to make any political statements in his music at this time, this was certainly an odd entry into Eno's catalogue of works and a track that has not been reissued in any form since, making it highly collectable for fans.

The track was also very confrontational for Eno's work during this period. Nylon had collected recordings of newscasts about the group and some static-driven German police telephone conversations featuring actual Baader-Meinhof ransom messages about the kidnapped Dutch industrialist Hanns Martin Schleyer. She asked Eno to provide some backing music for these which he was happy to do, and he raided some of the archives from 1975 to slowly start to piece together a backing track to these recordings (a technique he would utilise again four years later with David Byrne for the album *My Life In The Bush Of Ghosts*). Nylon and Palladin added some vocals to this, making the track an almost collage of material, all with an incredible fretless bass performance from Percy Jones, left over from *Another Green World* sessions. Nylon and Palladin's voices took on the role of passengers on what was a doomed Lufthansa plane, having a conversation while the terrorists walked around the aisles of the aircraft. The piece closed in an uncomfortable manner with a gunshot, someone shouting 'Heil' and a scream of 'No Sacrifice!'. It's an intense listening experience and something far more disturbing than anything that punk had been able to muster by this point; in fact, punk was already beginning to start its slow fade-out with the self-destruction of the genre's leaders the Sex Pistols in the USA.

One of Eno's first interviews of the year was with Kris Needs and Danny Baker for *ZigZag* magazine in January 1978, and here he discussed his inner creative turmoil that would be part of his almost creative stasis throughout the year:

What happened was when I first left Roxy, I had a very good time for a period because I was just available, you know. If someone was doing something interesting, they could ring and say they were doing this, do you want to join in? I really like joining in with things, you know. I'm not keen on permanently being in the role of thinking up the project, then getting it together, then organising it, all the work that goes into making a record, where you're involved in every stage from beginning to end. That way of working, which I've been doing now for a couple of years, has really drained my energy. That's why I enjoyed working on the Bowie things so much, because he was someone else with a lot of energy and with his own movement, which I could jump on to and slightly divert or follow, whichever I chose to do …

I rather think I fancy doing some things where I keep further back from being the focal point of what's happening, where I take a much more subsidiary role. I did those concerts with Fripp a couple of years ago, which I liked very much. It was one of the last things I did, which I really enjoyed a lot, and that was because what I did there was just provide a background for Fripp to work on, so I deliberately wasn't having a lead role.

These are interesting statements by Eno and set out fairly clearly what he thought he wanted to do during the course of 1978 and where he thought, or hoped, his career would eventually lead.

Eno started the new year in Conny Plank's studio in Wolperath, recording the delayed debut album by Devo called *Q: Are We Not Men? A: We Are Devo!*. The recording of the album was a torturous experience because not only were the band snowbound in the studio, but what was originally thought was going to be a happy working relationship soon turned fractious, as what the band wanted and what Eno did were at odds with each other. Eno wanted the band to experiment, but they wanted to rely on material they had from dozens of demo tapes they had brought along, making Eno, in the end, fall into line with what the band wanted.

There had been one bright ray of hope over the winter for Eno when he had met up again with Roedelius and Moebius at Plank's studio and the trio began working on new material, taking off from the same point their sessions had ended the previous year. Again, the three men improvised ideas and slowly built up sounds, with Plank adding extra effects on them from the control booth. The big difference between this and the previous recording was that Eno added some vocals on to three of the pieces that they recorded. Eventually, ten tracks were pulled from all the recording sessions and released in Germany only on Sky Records as *After The Heat*.

Eno, Moebius, Roedelius: After The Heat (1978)

Personnel:
Brian Eno: vocals, keyboards
Roedelius: keyboards
Moebius: keyboards
Holger Czukay: bass on 'Tzima N'Arki'
All songs written by Eno, Moebius, Roedelius
Produced by: Conny Plank, Eno, Moebius, Roedelius
Recorded at: Conny's Studio
Released by: Sky Records, Germany
Highest Chart Position: –
Tracklisting: Side One: 1. Oil, 2. Foreign Affairs, 3. Luftschloss, 4. The Shade, 5. Old Land, Side Two: 1. Base & Apex, 2. Light Arms, 3. Broken Head, 4. The Belldog, 5. Tzima N'Arki

The overall sound to the album is more experimental and a little less ambient in places. This can be seen in the first track, 'Oil' that has a jazz feel with some atonal synthesizer sounds playing over a simple piano motif. Rolling bass thunders underneath and cascading notes tumble over the top. It certainly lacks the serene feel of the first album. The track blends into 'Foreign Affairs' that has a stomping piano sound over which drifting synth pads and arpeggiated notes fight for attention. The sound of the synth here is reminiscent of the kind of voices Kraftwerk had used on *Trans Europe Express*, and all this makes for a fairly uptempo piece.

'Luftschloss' drags us back down to earth as it is largely a melancholy piano piece with synths swelling beneath to accentuate the atmosphere; it's here that you can reference the track that all three would work on *Before And After Science* as it has a similar feel. More melancholia in atmosphere is 'The Shade' with its plaintive piano notes drifting over a four-note synthesizer sequence that rises in tone as the song progresses. Its ending shifts chord sequences and sounds like the beginning of another track altogether. 'Old Land''s keyboards are haunting and restful as they swell and fade like waves on a beach, and the overall feel is one of calm reflection.

Side two starts with 'Base & Apex' and a more industrialised synth sound than on the previous side, with percussive elements clanking along with the chord structure. A mournful lead erupts at one point, almost sounding like a saxophone. 'Light Arms' is a slight one-and-a-half-minute piece that feels like a segue into the final part of the album that features three tracks with Eno's vocals on and some have commented they could have been *Before And After Science* tracks.

'Broken Head' has an oddly atonal pulsating rhythm that seems to randomly throw up synth notes around it. Eno discusses the lyrics in *More Dark Than Shark*:

I'm not sure where the phrase 'Broken Head' came from, except that it came from some obscure corner of my own broken head. Whether or not it was thus self-referential is a question best left to art historians and academics. I do recall at some time being aware that the lyric could be autobiographical, but that wasn't its conscious source.

'The Belldog' certainly fits the mood more of *Before And After Science*, as it is less atonal in construction than 'Broken Head' and has the bell-like sounds that are prevalent on the earlier album. Also, Eno's vocal stylings sound similar to that on his own solo album. The lyrics discuss machinery and man's relation to it and space. Some could almost sense that Eno was pulling a narrative from Fritz Lang's 1927 film *Metropolis*, and in fact, Russell Mills's later painting, illustrating the track, uses this as its inspirational kick-off point. The song meanders slightly like it was originally intended to be an instrumental piece that Eno then decided to add vocals over.

'Tzima N'Arki' ends the album with a fairly jerky reggae feeling over which Czukay adds some dub-style bass notes. The fact that the opening lyrics are the chorus to 'King's Lead Hat' backwards makes the song more self-referential than the other pieces recorded with Cluster. The lyrics are all reversed, so they sound like nonsense and make it impossible to extrapolate any real meaning from them as they sound like another instrument rather than a melody line.

On his notes for the 2009 reissue of the album, Asmus Tietchens says:

'After The Heat' is more of an Eno album bearing stylistic characteristics of Cluster music. Clearly, all three musicians inspired each other during their three weeks together without any clash of personalities. Nevertheless, some tracks sound more like Cluster, some more like Eno. So, it made perfect sense to collect the tracks with a Cluster flavour on 'Cluster & Eno' and the Eno-influenced material on 'After The Heat'. Signs of this division are evident on the album's English credits, with Eno's vocals on three tracks and his trademark AKS Synthi A sound.

The case can be argued for the reason why the credits are in English, but in my opinion, I don't think this is the greater influence of Eno on the album as the record would also only be available in the UK as an expensive import, this feels more like the label hoping it would shift a greater number of copies to Eno's UK and US fan base if they can clearly understand what the album is about and what is happening on it. This album also featured Eno's last lead vocal performance on record for over a decade, and the next time he would let his larynx run free would be on the Eno and Cale album *Wrong Way Up* that would be released in 1990.

In 1985 Sky released a compilation of their Eno and Cluster releases called *Old Land*, featuring nine tracks that were culled from the two albums, and this featured no new material but included a very ambient-looking photo taken by Michael Weisser.

While recording *After The Heat*, Eno found time to experiment on something for himself. He asked Christa Fast, who was Conny Plank's partner, and two other local female singers, Inge Zeininger and Christine Gomez, to record a series of vocal utterances; mainly, this consisted of a series of 'aaahhhs' that were said in harmony to a series of piano notes that Eno had recorded in the key of F minor. Eno then looped these recordings on huge lengths of tape that ran serpent-like around the studio to create a strangely alluring serene-type atmosphere that could be left to play for hours if the listener had wanted. This was an idea that Eno put in his memory bank and capitalised on at a future date as Eno would begin to view it as his follow-up, sound-wise, to *Discreet Music* with the sound of the taped voices shifting gradually, once played against each other on separate tape machines, slowly falling out of sync but creating a very special kind of ambience all of their own. Eno packed these recordings away, ready to use them when he would feel the inspiration strike him again.

There was no new studio album for Bowie either in 1978. Instead, the Thin White Duke embarked on his most extensive tour in three years, playing tracks mainly from *Low* and *Heroes*. Called the ISOLAR 2 tour, Bowie had originally approached Eno to join his band for the dates, especially as they would be starting the shows with 'Warszawa', a track Eno had pretty much written on his own. The set also featured the foot-tapping 'Sense Of Doubt', the atonal rush of 'Blackout' and the picturesque 'Art Decade'. Eno was certainly tempted to do the tour, as he and Bowie obviously got on well and they had fun together as well as creating great music. A mixture though of gruelling rehearsals and live schedules, as well as the possibility of very little improvisation, obviously made Eno recall his final months of live performances with Roxy Music and in the end, he turned down Bowie's invitation. Looking at the set list for the tour now, it's also hard to see what Eno would have added to Bowie standards such as 'The Jean Genie', 'Hang On To Yourself' and 'Suffragette City'.

When Bowie stepped out on stage in the UK with the neon strip lights behind him dressed in full Germanic Weimar mode with pegged trousers, immaculate make-up and a hairstyle reminiscent of 1930s Berlin, a whole group of the audience took note. The music of Bowie and Eno was new and electronic with a distinct European art-house feel to it, and even Bowie's older numbers had been slightly transformed to fit in with the new sound. This tour was the biggest influence on what would be the new music and style to come out of Britain in the early eighties. Rusty Egan and Steve Strange would start their Bowie 'Club For Heroes' night that later transformed its name to 'The Blitz Club' and created the name given to the movement it helped to start – 'The Blitz Kids' – also known as The New Romantics. By 1979 an alien-looking hybrid of Bowie and Eno covered in thick make-up and looking and singing coldly would reach number one in the charts with a 7" called 'Are Friends Electric?'. This was Gary Numan and his band Tubeway Army. It opened the floodgates to a plethora of electronic music artists and songs to start hitting the top ten of the UK singles chart for the next three-plus years; even Japan, a band started in 1974, began to have hits, their biggest being the Stockhausen-influenced 'Ghosts'. As for Bowie, he released a double live album of his tour later in 1978 under the name *Stage,* which cherry-picked tracks performed on the dates. Later in 2017, *Stage* was given a triple vinyl release putting tracks back in the order that they were performed live, adding songs that were not on the original vinyl release so the album was almost the entire show as performed on the ISOLAR 2 tour.

Stage would be seen as a stop-gap album before Bowie's next proper studio release, and the same could be said of Eno's *Music For Films* which also finally got a wider release during the year after its initial limited release in 1976. This time fewer tracks were on the album and Eno had added a few newer snippets and a different running order. The reviews were mainly positive, but they also discussed that the pieces were only very slight, some only lasting just over one minute, and how the record felt like it was putting a line under Eno's work for him to move on to his next stage. This, of course, is partly true; the album is not one that bears a lot of fruit from repeated listens due to the fact that many of the pieces feel like snippets, and hardly stay around long enough for the listener to immerse themselves in the atmosphere of a particular piece. Even its blank front cover and its rear with a blurred photo of Eno made the record seem like a rushed utilitarian release more aimed at the budget market (which it wasn't), similar to that of the ongoing 'Obscure Records' releases that petered to a halt during the course of the year, with its final release being Harold Budd's *Pavilion Of Dreams* album.

During March, Eno flew to the Bahamian Island of New Providence to begin work on the new Talking Heads album at Compass Point Studios. The recordings for the album were completed by late April and Eno then flew to New York to oversee the mastering of the album. He assumed that he would only be there for three weeks to see the mastering complete and take in some of the local atmosphere and music, but instead, Eno spent almost seven months in Manhattan taking time out from his own solo music, giving himself in some respects a little breathing space to reconsider what his next step would be.

By June of the year, Eno dropped hints about his next musical direction and had even already had the name for his next album. In an interview with Glenn O'Brien that month where he begins to discuss his new venture after being asked about structural approaches to music:

Yeah, but it's not released. There's a new series I've done of music designed for airports. It's called 'Music For Airports' in fact. I'm going to release it on my own label.

Now Eno began to settle himself into his adopted American lifestyle, and moved to Greenwich Village, spending his time going to galleries and to the cinema. In some respects, this gave him a mental breathing space even though he was still sought after for interviews with the music press. Eno also began to throw himself into the New York nightlife with clubs like Studio 54 and with the rise of the disco scene. The city had the feeling of the last days of the Roman Empire or of the decadence of Weimar-era Berlin. Eno even went to the club with Bowie when he was in town as part of his ISOLAR 2 tour. There were some who thought that Eno's move to New York was similar to that of Bowie's move to Berlin; it was for Eno to escape his rock past and hopefully move on from being labelled an 'ex-Roxy Music member' (something that still happens to this day).

In June, Eno was interviewed by Lisa Robinson of the *Daily Press*. Here we see a sense of self-deprecation as Eno is in the middle of his adjustment stateside, especially when asked about his collaboration with Bowie:

> It just happens that I'm in the interesting position of being neither a good producer nor a good musician. Anything complicated I do is done by ingenuity rather than skill, I think. People tend to panic when they get into a studio, perhaps because you can't see the electricity. To me, it's all playthings, really. The first thing I do about approaching any piece of technology is to hide the handbooks. I get those out of the way straight away.

This gives an interesting perspective on the way Eno thought of himself and worked with new pieces of studio equipment; for someone so keen on systems he was happy to leave things to happenstance when it actually came to the nuts and bolts of creating music.

At this point, Eno became fascinated with the plethora of new bands that began to spring up in New York in the wake of the great punk explosions there. Most gigs he attended were of this new wave of bands that were springing up and now beginning to saturate the live scene there. Many of these bands proclaimed themselves as 'non-musicians', something Eno himself had claimed five years earlier. The music was an assaultive barrage of atonal guitar noodling mixed with funk and jazz beats, all infused with the punk spirit. These were the post-Blondie and Talking Heads bands that saw even the Ramones start to become pop artists when they recorded with Phil Spector. They set themselves apart from the punk and new wave artists of the previous two years. The bands began to use the moniker 'no wave' to almost alienate themselves from what happened before. The band from the scene who went on to be the most well-known and remembered were Teenage Jesus And The

Jerks. This was largely down to their singer Lydia Lunch who pushed a genre-breaking and boundary-pushing career from 1980 onwards, being associated with such acts as The Birthday Party, Einstürzende Neubauten and the confrontational film-maker Richard Kern.

Eno had witnessed these bands at a benefit performance at the Fine Arts Building in Lower Manhattan in May 1978. Eno didn't really have to search out these new bands, as he stated later that he had had at least 200 demo tapes given to him since arriving in New York. Eno thought of the way he curated the Obscure artists and decided that he should try and get some of these bands into the studio to record a compilation of the scene at the time. He managed to sort out a cheap recording studio and then began to cherry-pick the bands he wanted to represent on the record. In the end, he only recorded four bands for the album. Of course, Eno chose Teenage Jesus And The Jerks, and they were joined by The Contortions, Mars and DNA, a band who had a Japanese girl drummer who couldn't play drums or speak English, and guitarist Arto Lindsay who would detune his 12-string guitar to make an atonal noise. DNA were almost perfect Eno fodder and probably reminded him of his days in the Portsmouth Sinfonia for their total lack of musicianship and vast amounts of attitude. Each band was allowed four songs on the album to showcase what they could do, and each band only had one day to record their numbers which, for at least two of the bands, was the first time they would have entered a studio.

The recording of the album wasn't easy, with some of the bands questioning Eno's commitment and integrity to the project (he was seen in the control booth reading the arts pages of the *New York Times* during the recording of Teenage Jesus). Some bands felt that Eno was trying to make a stateside name for himself for helming the project and trying to keep himself 'relevant' to the music scene in general. When Eno presented the tapes of the project to Island Records, they were both shocked and disinterested in the project. The only 'punk' bands the label had invested in were Ultravox! (who were predominantly art house) and Eddie And The Hot Rods, whose complicated fast playing was more in tune with The Who rather than the Sex Pistols. In the end, the label passed on the recordings for its own label, but they did finally see the light of day in November 1978 on their ancillary jazz label Antilles but were not released in the UK at all.

The reviews for the album were mixed, with many questioning Eno's actual input aside from pressing the record button. At least two of the bands featured split before the year was out and what seemed like a fecund music scene was already beginning to splinter and create something new, with bands like Sonic Youth borrowing from the sound but adding a touch of art rock to springboard their career. Because of his involvement in the project, the New York art set began to embrace Eno more than before, seeing him as a true avant-garde artist willing to still push a few boundaries.

To show that Eno had hit the New York scene big time, he was interviewed by Glenn O'Brien for the June issue of Andy Warhol's *Interview* magazine discussing Oblique Strategies, David Bowie, dub music, Donna Summer and Flying Saucers. Where the questions were fairly perfunctory ('Is it like muzak?' etc.), Eno gave good copy by giving long eloquent answers about his interests, working methods and possible future musical projects:

GO'B: On your last album, on Bowie's last few albums and on Kraftwerk's last two albums, there's danceable yet advanced music. Do you think about breaking through to the discos?
Eno: Oh yeah, I do. What I would really like to do, if I could have a sort of kingship for a short time and organize the group of my dreams – I would make one group which was a combination of, say, Parliament and Kraftwerk – put those two together and say, 'make a record'. Something like that would be an extraordinary combination; the weird physical feeling of Parliament, with this strange, rigid, stiff stuff over the top of it.

What Eno was describing was in fact, something he had heard the previous summer, which was Giorgio Moroder's song 'I Feel Love'. The discos, though, were not the place for Eno's solo music in the end, as already he was working his way towards soundscapes that would be in the opposite spectrum to any disco artist. Eno's stock was so high now that graffiti bearing the legend 'Eno Is God' started appearing on walls in downtown New York.

During this period, Eno contributed to Robert Fripp's first solo album being recorded in New York, which was released later that year with the title *Exposure*. The album was a mix of harder edge atonal guitar sounds and the more ambient side that he and Eno had explored a few years earlier. Fripp was now living in New York as well, and part of the reason that both men had relocated there was the amount of 'beautiful women' associated with the art scene and in the city in general. Eno had now shaken off his reclusive phase and was almost back to the galivanting musician of that first Roxy US tour.

In late September, Eno flew via London to Montreux in Switzerland to begin work on his next collaboration with Bowie and what was his final album working with him. Bowie had just finished his tour and wanted to use some of the musicians from his band on the album while they were still rehearsed, red hot and immersed in Bowie's mindset. The making of this album and its release the following year I will discuss in the next chapter.

Eno returned to New York before Christmas with hundreds of demo tapes posted through his letter box. Into a barrage of musical proposals, in a strange way, all this information began to overwhelm Eno, who almost wanted to do as many as he could but then would also be letting other projects remain fallow. The volume of proposals made it hard for Eno to move forward with his own ongoing work, as he found himself stuck with too many interesting projects. For Eno feeling himself in stasis, he did what he would always do either by fate of accident or choice, but this time it was by choice. Eno decided to put himself in a strange location he had never been before, hoping that it would kick-start his creativity again and give him head space from the bombardment of requests. On Christmas Day 1978, Eno flew out to Bangkok to reinvigorate himself, and travelling with only a few possessions, he obviously felt that this would help him shake off the baggage that was overwhelming him in America.

Ambient Records, Music For Airports, Lodger 1979

Even though most of the music in this chapter was recorded in 1978, the records would not be released until 1979, so it seemed sensible to discuss the contents and the making of it on the year that they were released. However, although some people, including Sheppard mention that *Music For Airports* was released in 1978, I can find no reviews of the album at that time and checking on Discogs, it clearly states that the album was released in 1979, even though the album sleeve itself says 1978. This discrepancy must be due to the fact that Island was originally going to release the record in 1978, but somehow the record, yet again, got delayed. Even the recent remastered reissue of the album has its release date as 1978 on the sleeve. But because of the evidence on Discogs and the lack of reviews in 1978, I am going to assume that it was in fact a 1979 release in the UK March 1979, and later in other regions.

By the beginning of 1979, Eno was already telling interviewers that he had given up writing songs and that he found lyrics and his own vocal performances less interesting at this point. In fact, 1979 was a the year when Eno took over the curatorship of ambient music and pulled in musicians and artists that gave an overall uniformity to it as both the music and Eno entered the 1980s. It is unclear at this point whether Eno viewed his Ambient catalogue of music as just a couple of releases or, like Obscure Records, a plethora of releases featuring different artists. In the end, the Ambient label only released four records, three of them with Eno as composer. It is strange to think why he had given up on the label so quickly, especially as the uniform album covers for the releases were certainly more eye-catching than the Obscure releases.

Eno returned to New York from sampling the delights of Thailand at the end of February 1979. He felt there was a change in the atmosphere, a shift in feeling that had happened within the two months he was away, and suddenly within those couple of months, the world had shifted on its axis slightly and had left Eno slightly behind. Eno still had work to do, though, as he joined both Bowie and Visconti at Record Plant studios to work on a final mix of the album *Lodger*. Reports began to surface that there were arguments between the three men during the sessions, something that Bowie later denied, but it would take him 16 years before he would work with Eno again.

In March, Eno started to work as producer on the next Talking Heads album, the last that he would work on with the band, and the record that was a significant game-changer for them. It's around this time that *Music For Airports* finally got released in the UK. Billed as 'Ambient 1', it already hinted at maybe several volumes that would follow it. Its gestation had begun a year earlier while Eno was recording with Cluster in Germany. It was later in the year that he would work on these recordings in Basing Street Studios, London, adding more 'samples' of sound and instruments into the mix to create four elongated, languid pieces of music that could drift past the listener if need be.

The idea for the record had already begun to formulate in Eno's brain earlier while he was waiting for a flight inside the Cologne-Bonn International Airport in Germany. Oddly the structure had been designed by Paul Schneider-Esleben, the father of Kraftwerk's Florian Schneider. Eno thought that the building had a certain ambient coolness to it that he felt put travellers at ease before boarding their flights. But what was missing from the building was the right kind of music that would have an extra calming soporific effect on the passengers. This music would have to be both noticeable and unobtrusive at the same time. It wasn't until Eno had started recording the 'aaahhhs' in the studio during the *After The Heat* sessions that he felt he could create something that would do the building that inspired him justice. *Music For Airports* would be the gateway album for Eno and it would be the release that underlined most of his early eighties output in the way of feel and atmosphere.

Back in Basing Street Studios, Eno called on the services of both Fred Frith and Robert Wyatt to begin to fill out the tracks he had recorded in Cologne. Wyatt was told to play spontaneously, according to an interview he did with Sheppard:

> Brian just sort of got me to improvise at the piano for a while and chose what to use later. I was surprised and delighted with his use of what I did – how he created a sustained mood. I didn't know what he would do with what I'd played … I think the results were brilliant, pure Brian – great stuff!

Fred Frith played some guitar scrapes and some bass notes and Rhett Davies played the Fender Rhodes piano, sprinkling odd notes here and there. None of the musicians could hear what the others were playing, and Eno assembled all these performances like a collage over the backing track of voices adding his usual plentiful echo and reverb. Eno was particularly taken with a section of Wyatt's performance where he played six notes that almost seemed ethereal. He cut this part out, made a stereo loop of it and had it gently repeating at almost half its speed so that the notes had a kind of soporific sound to them as they rang out over each other. The finished results of all this stretched into a 16-and-a-half-minute track that took up most of side one of the LP. Eno embellished the piece with some synthesizer chords to add to the overall feeling of tranquillity of the piece. A further piece was worked on that day with Eno adding notes from his ARP synthesizer, which hung in the air, creating an atmosphere of total bliss for both intense listener and those that would be passive at its desired location.

In an interview with Lester Bangs for *Musician* magazine in November 1979, Eno discussed what he was aiming for with this music:

On the one hand, the music sounds to me very emotional, but the emotions are confused, they're not straightforward: in things that are very uptempo and frenzied there's nearly always a melancholy edge somehow. What people call unemotional just doesn't have a single overriding emotion to it. Certainly, the things that I like best are the ones that are the most sort of ambiguous on the emotional level. Also, one or two of the pieces I've made have been attempts to trigger that sort of unnervous stillness where you don't feel that for the world to be interesting you have to be manipulating it all the time.

Eno was into making small interferences in time for people, a moment, or 16, where they could step out of their everyday environment and maybe somehow notice it in a different way. It would still be the same view from the window that they looked at constantly, but now they could set aside some space and time to notice the small changes in light and movement as if the world becomes a painting and the music allows you to step back and admire the whole piece rather than see the frantic marks of the paintbrush that go into the creation of the work. This was also the beginning of a change of perception in the kind of music maker that the public would view Eno as; suddenly, he emerged as a maker of utility music as far away from his glam rock beginnings as Satie was to the Sex Pistols.

In fact, *Music For Airports* is far more connected to the work of Steve Reich, Philip Glass and John Cage than any type of rock aesthetic. This is Eno finally embracing his minimalist heroes from the early seventies, the composers and musicians who inspired him before he landed in the rock world with Roxy Music. Some have argued that the album is a continuation of his work on *Discreet Music,* but if that was truly the case, then surely it would also have been released as an 'Obscure' album and nicely bookended the series. *Music For Airports* also became Eno's bestselling album in America and would have certainly fitted in well with the minimalism in music that was all the rage with the art-house set at that period of time. The pieces also reference Stockhausen within their use of space as well, something that was certainly absent from Glass's use of arpeggios.

Eno was interviewed about his work in *Melody Maker* in late 1979 by Richard Williams, that was printed in the 12 January issue, where he mentions the thought process for *Music For Airports*:

When you're in the studio, the things that convince you that you're achieving something are the things that give you this charge of energy. When you're doing something like 'Music For Airports', it's so laid-back that it's hard to convince yourself that you're doing anything. It's not until you take it home and realise that you really enjoy it, and that that's the mood you want from music ... something as slow as that.

The album was also played at gallery installations as it was the perfect music for people to maybe look at the art on display in different ways. This aspect of making the music almost utilitarian is also played out on the track titles, which are the numbers they would have been on the original vinyl, examples being 1/1 and for side two 2/2, which takes away from the listener putting any preconceived notions of linear thought within either a statement or story on to the music as its playing or while staring at the sleeve. Beneath each title on the sleeve is either a form of modern classical notation or a waveform depending upon from which perspective you are looking at it. On the insert to the album, Eno points out the difference between his work and 'muzak', the kind of music piped into lifts and department stores:

Over the past three years, I have become interested in the use of music as ambience and have come to believe that it is possible to produce material that can be used thus without being in any way compromised. To create a distinction between my own experiments in this area and the products of the various purveyors of canned music, I have begun using the term Ambient Music.

This became Eno's statement of intent and one that took him into the next decade, where he pretty much abandoned creating anything with a rock aesthetic to it. In fact, Eno's intention was to create music that was as easily ignorable as it was listenable and in most cases, he succeeded in doing so without relying too heavily on classic melodic structures. Ambient music was now fully formed with a clear distinction from other musics and its own artistic manifesto laid down by Eno; this then enticed other musicians to follow his lead to creating music with low-event horizons. We also have to remember that this album was being released in the aftermath of punk and would be predominantly reviewed by the rock music press. In the 21st century, Ambient music is now everywhere and is used by dance artists etc. In 1979 this was a very different prospect and Eno's album fell in between the cracks of modern classical and rock music purely because of Eno's association with rock.

Brian Eno: Music For Airports (1979)

Personnel:
Brian Eno: synthesizer, treatments, concept
Robert Wyatt: piano (track 1)
Fred Frith: guitar (track 1)
Christa Fast, Christine Gomez, Inge Zeininger: voices (tracks 2/1, 1/2)
Produced by: Brian Eno, Rhett Davies
Engineer: Conny Plank, David Hutchins
All songs written by Brian Eno unless stated
Released: March 1979
Highest Chart Position: –
Tracklisting: Side One: 1. 1/1 (Eno, Wyatt), 2. 2/1. Side Two: 1. 1/2, 2. 2/2

Music For Airports became one of Eno's bestselling albums and it was something the people who bought it understood more so than the critics at the time. It was also quite rare for an album that is so musically static to sell in such large quantities, so maybe this was a quiet revolution against two years of punk's aggression and disco's constant beat. It is also a very hard album to discuss within the context of rock music, as many writers' rather brief reviews of the album at the time of release also stumbled at this. Lots of the reviews were fairly negative, some accusing Eno of either disappearing up his own posterior or describing the music as 'cold', 'emotionless' and 'dull', obviously totally missing the point of the function of the music. It was also at this point that the term Eno-esque was being used as a put-down argument by the *NME* for some artists, and the most noticeable of these were the bands now emerging from the Blitz Club coterie.

To talk about it track by track is very difficult as so little happens within the context of the actual music that it becomes almost meaningless to talk about individual tracks. Especially as one track is just two separate pieces that are overlayed over each other, which is not something new to Eno as recycling bits of music has been a constant with him in one form or another and the piecing of the two tracks makes perfect sense in the overall feeling and atmosphere that Eno is trying to evoke with the work.

Eric Tamm, in his 1995 book *Brian Eno; His Music and the Vertical Colour of Sound,* discusses one of the pieces:

2/1, the second piece on the first side, is the purest, and arguably the most effective, of the four compositions. The only sound sources are taped female voices singing single pitches on the syllable 'ah' with an absolutely unwavering tone production for about five seconds per pitch. These sung notes have been electronically treated to give them a soft attack/decay envelope and a slight hiss that accompanies the tone. Once again, the pitch material is very limited: seven tones that, taken together, spell a D major seventh chord with an added ninth.

In John T Lysaker's 2019 book *Brian Eno's Ambient 1: Music For Airports* by Oxford University Press, he discusses the work within the broader concept of modern classical music, such as Satie and Glass, rather than from a rock perspective, then focuses on the meaning of Ambient:

Eno imagines a more flexible catalogue of works. Moreover, he does not limit ambient music to the background; that is just one of its possible functions. 'Ambient Music must be able to accommodate many levels of listening attention without enforcing one in particular.' Bertin's diverse analogies seem more apropos to Eno's efforts, therefore, than to Satie's. Finally, in imagining its impress – what it does to us – Eno conceives of something more specific than light; a tint, hence Eno's emphasis on mood. Eno associates MFA with a sense of calm, which I take to be more than the simple absence of anxiety; it connotes a readiness, even serenity.

This serenity is key to the album and was designed to put travellers at ease; the fact that the music was played, or piped, into the sound system of LaGuardia airport at its Marine Terminal during a month in 1980 proved that this was as experimental for Eno as any work by Cage or Stockhausen. The music was also used by a number of other airports throughout 1980. Unfortunately, there are no reports to say whether passengers were more at ease while waiting for their flights while the soporific tones of Eno's music is played. It is odd to note that in recent times certain airports, such as one in Rome etc., have placed pianos near the boarding terminals for passengers to play if they so wish to calm themselves before a flight. In 1998 the music ensemble Bang On A Can performed the entire album live at an airport in Holland, with the sound of the loudspeakers announcing flights becoming part of the music, which in some sense was getting closer to Cage's way of making music, allowing whatever noises that were happening in and around the concert hall to be incorporated into the performance.

In the *Enovations* newsletter from the summer of 1979, Eno writes about his reactions to the lukewarm music press at the album's release and discusses the album's conception:

Airports was done with a minimum of good intentions; I didn't go into it thinking I'm going to make a very interesting piece of music here. I went in thinking I just wanted to make something that would work in an airport, that would actually make you think that flying was a pleasant thing to do instead of an unbearably uncomfortable thing, as it generally is. The particular piece I'm referring to was done by using a series of very long tape loops, like 50, 60, 70 feet long. There were 22 loops. One loop had just one piano note on it. Another would have two piano notes. Another would have a group of girls singing one note, sustaining it for ten seconds. There are eight loops of girls' voices and about 14 loops of piano. I just set all of these loops running and let them configure in whichever way they wanted to, and in fact, the result is very, very nice. The interesting thing is that it doesn't sound at all mechanical or mathematical as you would imagine, it sounds like some guy is sitting there playing the piano with quite intense feeling. The spacing and the dynamics of 'his' playing sound very well organised. That was an example of hardly interfering at all.

Music For Airports stands as being the first-ever official 'ambient' album ever made, something that by the early nineties would be ubiquitous in most music stores and charts across the world.

It is interesting to note that Eno had created music to be played in a location that his friend Bowie would never experience. For Bowie, flying was a big no-no at this point and like some rich traveller from the earlier part of the twentieth century, he would only travel by liner, and this included while on tour, so that dates in the US, for instance, had to be booked sometime after European shows so that Bowie could travel by sea to his next location.

There were no such watery travel problems for Bowie when he called Eno to the Mountain Studio in Montreux to begin work on their next collaboration together that would be titled *Lodger*. Even though the album was lumbered under the collective title of 'the Berlin trilogy', it was the only album that did not even touch the sides of the Berlin Wall in its production. By this point, Bowie was beginning to move on from the austere landscapes and the city itself that had so strongly influenced his previous two albums, and by the finish of the mixing for *Lodger* he also moved on from Eno as well and oddly took on a mixture of New York art rock and London Blitz Club feel for his first album of the eighties.

Even though Bowie used the same musicians that he had on *Low* and *Heroes*, he also added members of his ISOLAR 2 touring band, which included Simon House and ex-Frank Zappa (and soon to be King Crimson) guitarist Adrian Belew. The first problem was that the guitar had lost some of the subtlety that Fripp brought to the table on *Heroes*, with Belew's guitar being on full assault mode for large sections of the album. The general consensus among critics at the time was that *Lodger* was the weakest of the three 'Berlin' albums, with Belew's guitar work being singled out as part of the reason for this.

At the start of the recording, Eno had played Bowie the new Walker Brothers album *Nite Flights* that had four of Scott Walker's most visceral pieces of music on it. Both Bowie and Eno agreed that this was a direction they would be willing to investigate for the album that, at this point, had the working title 'Planned Accidents'.

In the planning stages for the record, both Bowie and Eno agreed that the album would be split again between a vocal side and an instrumental side. However, as recording progressed, Bowie was coming up with more lyrics than he had done on the previous two albums, so the whole idea of having an instrumental side was then shelved in favour of the songs. Bowie was writing songs about being geographically displaced, something he was again now his Berlin tenancy had run its natural course, so side one of the album was taken over with songs about this state of mind and life, whereas side two songs was about Western life in general (Bowie had already hinted that he would like to move to Japan at this point), and these songs are more of a critique of what European living was like in Bowie's mind.

Again, Visconti was at the mixing desk and he and Eno began to discuss the album as 'hybridism' or a form of proto-world music, something that Eno would investigate a year later with trumpeter Jon Hassell on his *Fourth World Vol 1: Possible Musics* album. Eno filtered these ethnic sounds and ideas by adding some funk (similar to what he did with Talking Heads) and, of course, rock and his arsenal of electronic effects that gave the album a slightly odd, misplaced feeling. In the end, Eno was credited as co-writing six of *Lodger*'s ten songs. This was Bowie's travelogue album. After two records constrained by being separated from the world surrounded by the Berlin Wall, Bowie wanted to stretch his wings, and musical styles to make an album that revealed him as being part of the new jet set, even though he had never set foot on a plane. This idea of travel being exotic for an artist was taken up by the new vanguard of pop/rock artists, and most noticeably among these would be David Sylvian, who would capitalise on the idea of being the displaced artist referencing exotic countries but in a way of a tortured poet viewing these places but not really interacting with them.

Thomas Jerome Seabrook discusses the initial recording sessions in his book *Bowie In Berlin*:

Bowie worked with Carlos Alomar, Dennis Davis and George Murray on rhythm tracks. Eno was also present from the start; Sean Mayes and Simon House came in a few days later, first to join in on spontaneous full-band recordings and then to add overdubs to backing tracks looped and edited by Bowie and Visconti. The last musician to arrive was Adrian Belew who was put through the same ordeal Robert Fripp had been on 'Heroes': that is, he was simply told to start playing without having heard any of the songs.

It has been noted that the core of the album was a sense of repetition (even one of the songs is called that), with this similar set-up, it seems that Bowie and Eno were going for the 'if it isn't broken, don't fix it' methodology. This is odd for Eno because he would normally push artists to go beyond their comfort boundaries to confront something different, but here we see a similar way of working that happened on the previous two albums.

Visconti noted that Eno had grown in confidence as a collaborator and producer, and this was put down to the fact that his work with Talking Heads had been highly praised and the fact that Bowie had mentioned wanting to get some of that 'Heads' vibe on to the new album. Visconti said that during the recording of *Lodger*, Eno was 'very much in control'. Eno was bringing in conceptual ideas, but most of these would be unused on the album. One of these was Eno bringing in a blackboard and writing his eight favourite chords on it. He would say to the rhythm section that he would like them to play a 'funky groove' and using a teacher's pointer, he would point at the chords and tell the musicians to change to the next notes he pointed at after four beats; Alomar was less than impressed with this technique.

Again, Oblique Strategies were employed, but they seemed to have a lesser effect on the sound of the album than on previous records. It was, however, this high-concept way of working that began to cause a rift between Bowie and Eno. Bowie certainly had always been a control freak so maybe he began to feel that Eno was slowly hijacking his album in some way and tensions grew between them as the recording went on. Gone was the humour of the recording process of *Heroes* as a more sombre atmosphere pervaded over the studio. The pair never visibly argued in front of the other musicians (well, they both denied doing so), but Bowie once commented that 'Artistic temper sort of shows, I think the way we solve it is that one or the other will leave the studio for a couple of hours and let the other get on with it ...'

This tension can be seen in two ways: because of the success of the previous two albums, the expectations on both Bowie and Eno to create another work of genius was hanging heavy on their shoulders. We have to remember that when Eno attended the *Low* sessions, Bowie was even unsure whether the recordings would be released, so the pressure was already off creatively, leaving them open to explore whatever they wanted to musically. The reason could be that Bowie, always the most impulsive of people, was beginning to find the high concepts that Eno was bringing to the studio somewhat tiring. Bowie constantly kept an eye on what was happening musically so that he could somehow stay ahead of the game, something he had been pretty successful at doing for the last seven years. It seemed Bowie was growing fatigued with the conceptual way of working and was already thinking of his next move ahead and what that should be. In a strange way *Lodger* does feel like a stopgap record for Bowie, one where he is almost treading water until the next bolt of genius would hit his creative brow. A year later, in an *NME* interview, Bowie would distance himself from the conceptual way of working and would even call Eno's *Music For Airports* album 'unremittingly dull'.

Still, there was some fun to be had during the recordings as well, as Eno would get the musicians to swap instruments: he himself would be at the piano playing a basic chord sequence, Alomar played drums, Davis played bass and Murray was on keyboards. Here they created a proto-punk and funk piece that was originally christened 'Louis Reed', but which was later renamed 'Boys Keep Swinging' and was released as the first single from the album. This is one of the concepts that worked particularly well on the album and later, Bowie made the wonderful cross-dressing promo video to accompany the song's release.

Another concept that Eno brought into play during the recording was the use of backing tracks of some of Bowie's old songs but played in reverse, and it is here that the chord progression to 'All The Young Dudes' becomes the track 'Move On'. It is hard to say what Bowie thought of this plundering of his past in such a dramatic way, but with what appears to be no actual songs written before hitting the studio, it seems that both Bowie and Eno were 'winging it' in some ways to meet a deadline and to get new Bowie product on the market as soon as possible after the critical success of his ISOLAR 2 tour. Also, Bowie and his band were on a tight schedule as the Australian end of his tour was about to start as well, which would leave Eno and Visconti to mop up any end pieces of the recording process, including editing together Belew's guitar parts that he had to blind to each track with only three attempts allowed at each song. Eno and Visconti pieced together the guitar parts from these three separate recordings much as they had done with Fripp's work on the *Heroes* album. Eno once expressed in the 1980s that 'there's nothing more certain to kill an idea than democracy, as far as I'm concerned. If you are going to make an experiment, just make it.' This could be Eno referring to the experience of making *Lodger*.

One thing of note was the protracted recording and mixing compared to the previous albums that were knocked out in a fever pitch of energy so that the musicians were all on a high, fuelled by the new material. This way of working suited Bowie well as he tended to get bored or distracted when studio time dragged on because he was used to working quickly. Even the release schedules were different, with both *Low* and *Heroes* coming out within quite a short time, whereas *Lodger* would still be tinkered with some six months later with Bowie re-recording some vocals and Visconti replacing Davis' bass part on 'Boys Keep Swinging'. This was a snail's pace for a Bowie album, even though he had been on tour during part of its creation.

Paul Yamada discusses how *Lodger* was different from its predecessors in an article from the *New York Rocker* in July 1979:

> Compared to 'Low' and 'Heroes' this is more than a retreat. 'Lodger' simply uses electronics, dissonance and thick textures. It does not allow them to do any independent work, to carry any weight by themselves. The songs are ordinary by Bowie's recent standards; they say little, have slight content, and hide behind exotic and foreign circumstances. The true 'lodger', the refugee from everywhere, would have more to say, more at stake, and could never be so passionless, so facile. There is still good music here, well played, unusual, once in a while excellent. The LP is easy to listen to because it rarely challenges the listener, it only baits you with slick and highly embossed surfaces. It is not really a departure from 'Low' and 'Heroes', but a rejection of their serious nature.

This sounds quite harsh, but at the time, many reviewers and people who bought the record complained about the muddy mix of sound on the album. Also, many people were expecting it to be more of a challenging record in the same way that *Low* almost emerged from nowhere and took people by surprise, which is something that both Bowie and Eno could have never really pulled off for a third time, especially with the amount of expectation on them.

David Bowie: Lodger (1979)

Personnel:
David Bowie: vocals, synthesizer, piano, Chamberlin, guitar
Brian Eno: piano, synthesizer, horse trumpet and eroica horn, treatments, backing vocals, ambient drone
Tony Visconti: mandolin, guitar, bass, backing vocals
Adrian Belew: guitar, mandolin
Carlos Alomar: guitar, drums, backing vocals
Dennis Davis: drums, bass, backing vocals
George Murray: bass, backing vocals
Sean Mayes: piano
Simon House: violin, mandolin, backing vocals
Roger Powell: synthesizers

Stan Harrison: saxophone
All songs by Bowie except tracks 1, 6, 7, 8 Bowie and Eno, and 10 Bowie and
Alomar
Produced by: David Bowie and Tony Visconti
Recorded at: Mountain Studios
Mixed at: Record Plant, New York City
Released: 18 May 1979
RCA Records
Highest Chart Position: UK: 4; US Billboard: 20
Tracklisting: Side One: 1. Fantastic Voyage, 2. African Night Flight, 3. Move
On, 4. Yassassin, 5. Red Sails Side Two: 1. DJ, 2, Look Back In Anger, 3. Boys
Keep Swinging, 4. Repetition, 5. Red Money

For review purposes, I am using Visconti's 2017 vinyl remix of the album
because the sound quality is less muddy on this mix.

Before the music, it's the cover that hits you first. This is Bowie's most
audacious sleeve and the first studio album to have a gatefold sleeve by
him. The photograph that adorns the front was based on self-portraits by
the artist Egon Schiele that Bowie greatly admired. The design was done
by British artist Derek Boshier and photographed by Brian Duffy. Bowie
looks like he has been hit by a car with his face made to look flattened by
prosthetics. He lies in an awkward position on a tiled floor, I'm assuming
that the design was OK'd before the album was renamed *Lodger,* as it fits
in with the original title 'Planned Accidents' better.

'Fantastic Voyage' is a typical laid-back Bowie tune that pointed more
towards his mid-eighties style than fitting in with the kind of songwriting
of the previous albums. The song is a rather delicate number compared to
the opening of *Low* and *Heroes,* its rolling bass and piano lines managing
to give a sense of serenity and possibly pointing the way towards this
being a less intense work than its predecessors. 'African Night Flight' has
the kind of rhythm section that Eno would lift wholesale for the album
he would make with David Byrne in 1981, *My Life In The Bush Of Ghosts.*
Its synth sounds play awkwardly beneath this rhythm, making the piece
sound fairly atonal and Bowie gives one of his most restrained vocal
performances. There are elements of Talking Heads in its soundscape, but
it does sound like both Bowie and Eno threw the kitchen sink at it sound-
wise, with instruments fighting to be heard over the clatter, and this seems
like more of an Eno piece just because of the type of experimentation that
happens during the piece.

'Move On' is the 'Young Dudes' backwards track, so it sounds more like Bowie of old in its construction. Here Bowie ruminates on his travelogue of places he's visited, but the whole track lacks a sense of urgency and never really peaks in any particular way. It is odd for an album that Eno is said to have a large part in creating that so far, his performance on it is not as noticeable as on the previous albums. 'Yassassin' is what used to be referred to as a cod reggae track that mixes in a little funk and uses Simon House's violin to conjure up some Middle Eastern folk tunes over the top. This makes the track feel slightly muddled and you can almost feel the lack of interest in Bowie's voice as he borrows Turkish motifs in his vocal delivery. 'Red Sails' is the strongest song on the first side, and borrowing its motoric beat from 'Neu!' it feels like Bowie and Eno's last tip of the hat to the Berlin days while the vocal melody hints at a Japanese approach, something that would be taken further on the next album. Again, there is an old amalgamation of cultural references that collide to make the track something of an oddity.

Side two would produce three singles from the album as RCA was trying to keep interest going in the record after some fairly negative reviews. This makes side two seem stronger musically because the songs seem more geared to being single releases, although I doubt it was intentional. 'DJ' Bowie later admitted was his 'natural response to disco'. Its steady repetitive melody really picks in its chorus, which lifts the song away from being rather simplistic. Bowie's Chamberlin adds a suitable atonal fare over proceedings. This is an Eno co-written song where he doesn't appear on any of the instruments being performed. 'Look Back In Anger' is an excellent propulsive rock song with an element of the old Berlin feel about it. Another Eno co-write, you can clearly hear his rumbling synthesizer giving the track its bottom end. It's the track that most feels like the successor to pieces on *Heroes,* with its strong rhythm section and snappy guitar fugue adding to the heady brew mixture of the song.

The hit single and most well-known track from the album and another Eno co-write, 'Boys Keep Swinging' seems to point in some respects towards Bowie's next album before he does his next chameleon change into an eighties pop star. The song is big and brash, with a slight underlying camp element all thrown into the boiling pot. It is the most glam rock-sounding song that either Bowie or Eno had produced since 1974 and feels like the two men trying to enjoy themselves and have fun as they did in the old days before art concepts began to weigh them down. 'Repetition' has a queasy kind of sound with some ill-sounding guitar and a strange bass melody that plays at odds with the other instruments. Again, Eno plays no instruments on this track, so one can only surmise that his input would have been on the conceptual side, and the track is reminiscent of songs that The Stranglers produced on their 1978 album *Black and White*. 'Red Money' seems to have borrowed part of the backing track from 'Sister Midnight' that Iggy Pop recorded for his Bowie-produced album *The Idiot*. New guitar sounds were added, as well as Roger Powell's synth sounds that battle it out over a slight funk rhythm. Again, Eno is conspicuous in his absence of playing on this track.

Tony Visconti once said that Bowie's heart really wasn't into the making of the album. Also, for a project that Eno is meant to have had more control over, he only actually appears on roughly half the tracks on the record and is even absent on some he co-wrote. It is difficult to ascertain now exactly what was happening during the recording process and how much Eno had asserted his will over the recordings, or certainly the tracks that were used. It is sad that the duo's last album together for the decade would be such a muddled affair, and one that neither seemed very happy or positive about in the end. Maybe it's the fact that the location of where the previous albums were recorded had bled through into the pair's creativity, something that Switzerland had failed to do in some way artistically for both musicians. The eighties would see Bowie drift away from experimentation as he tried to reinvent himself. Whereas before, he had always stayed one step ahead, by the mid-eighties he had seemed to be usurped from being 'the one to watch' for music's future direction.

For Eno, though, 1979 would see one more art-house style release, and this would be in the form of a limited-numbered Spanish-only release album that he performed and wrote the music for with King Crimson and Emerson Lake and Palmer wordsmith (and the first Roxy album producer) Pete Sinfield. The album called *Robert Sheckley's In A Land Of Clear Colors* would become one of the most sought-after Eno projects over the years. Sinfield is the narrator and reads Sheckley's text about an intergalactic exile who adapts himself to the ways of the planet on which he has been marooned. The album would be released in 1,000 copies only by an art gallery Galeria el Mensajero and it was presented in a slipcase containing a book with art by Leonor Quiles. The original metal masters for the album were allegedly destroyed, although the label Voiceprint put out a limited 'remastered' CD copy in 1993. Since then, the record has not been rereleased in any format, so even these CDs now fetch a fairly hefty price tag on the second-hand market.

By the end of the summer of 1979, Eno was beginning to think about his own next solo album and where he should go next musically. He had boldly announced that *Music For Airports* would be Ambient Number 1 but had so far not been able to create 'number two' or find a suitable artist to produce to carry on his ambient legacy in much the same way he had done with the Obscure label.

He had heard the album *Vernal Equinox* by Jon Hassell, a jazz trumpeter who mixed avant-garde playing with a strange kind of tribalism to produce a strange ethereal sound that had peaked Eno's interest so much that out of his own money, he booked a studio to create a similar kind of rhythmic feel. It was at this point that he was introduced to Hassell and the pair started making notes about recording an album together, blending the type of world music that Eno had been experimenting with Bowie with that of jazz and electronica. Eno first started to record his own solo album and pulled in Talking Heads drummer Chris Franz along with several New York buskers to start laying down the rhythm tracks. One of these buskers was a zither player Edward Larry Gordon who soon became known under the name Laraaji. Laraaji would later be the only musician to record a solo album for Eno's Ambient imprint recording his album *Day Of Radiance,* which was released in 1980. Also brought along for the sessions was David Byrne, Pere Ubu and Bill Laswell, so this was Eno playing ringmaster to lots of disparate musicians in a similar way as he had done five years earlier with *Here Come The Warm Jets.* Eno had become obsessed with short-wave radio and began recording some of the odd programmes that he heard on it and taking what we would now call samples, of broadcasts he liked and cutting them up to fit over the rhythm patterns that he had recorded in the studio. These recordings would become the nucleus for *My Life In The Bush Of Ghosts,* an album that would transform what was one of the first to use entirely found sounds alongside artists such as Holger Czukay, who used a similar variation using Dictaphones.

But before he could continue work on his album, Eno had to start recording Hassell's album. Eno's first port of call was to phone Fripp to get him to play some guitar work for the record. Hassell had wanted to expand his sound away from the basic instrumentation of his first album and also get away from using purely traditional instrumentation to add drones beneath his playing. Here Eno gave him washes of ambient synth playing that Hassell could begin to extemporise over. Adding Fripp into the mix of it seemed like a good idea at the time, the problem being that both Fripp and Eno began to settle into their usual style of recording, with Fripp using his Frippertronics guitar style over Eno's soundscapes. This made the pair realise that they were actually recording a new Fripp and Eno album rather than a backing for Jon Hassell. They decided that they would call this album *Music For Healing*, and now the only surviving track from this album is 'Healthy Colours parts 1–4' that wouldn't see a release until 1994 as part of the compilation album *Essential Fripp & Eno*. Here again, Eno used found vocal sources to layer over Fripp's guitar work, pointing more towards Eno's obsession at the time probably more than Fripp's. This sound was a big departure from their previous releases. Maybe at some point, the rest of the recordings will emerge from these sessions.

Eno decided not to use any of the music recorded so far for use on the Hassell project and reconvened to start again, using Brazilian percussionist Nana Vasconcelos and his old friend Percy Jones on bass. Eno added treatments, guitars and synthesizer over these rhythmic pieces and Hassell then added his enigmatic trumpet playing over the top of these washes of sound. The record was released the following year under the titles *Fourth World Vol 1 – Possible Musics*, the title, like the ambient series, hints at future releases but in the end only one further 'Fourth World' album would be released. The big mystery was why the album was never released as *Ambient 2* as the sound of the record certainly wouldn't have been out of place with what became the ambient catalogue. Hassell later admitted that he was unhappy about it being released as an Eno & Hassell album and felt it should have been put out as more of a solo project with Eno being credited for production and for what instrumentation that he actually played on the album. The album was released to little fanfare in March 1980 but has since become heralded as one of the most important albums of ambient music and has become a major influence on other artists working in the same area, most noticeably David Sylvian, who would get Hassell to help almost recreate the sound on one of his solo albums.

Around this time, Eno purchased a second-hand video camera with an idea of making some type of visual art that could be screened alongside his music. Cameras at that time were large and cumbersome instruments that could also be unreliable and idiosyncratic. Eno decided he was going to start off filming the view from his New York apartment window and he placed the camera there to film, but because he had not bought a tripod to place it on, the camera would fall on its side as it was recording.

DECADES | Brian Eno in the 70s

Eno would let it 'do its thing' while he busied himself around the flat. Through another piece of Eno happenstance, he found during playback that the camera, because of its vertical recording, had revealed more of the sky than if it had remained horizontal. Turning his TV on its side, Eno watched the slow-moving of clouds over the Manhattan skyline giving more of an essence of a painting than a movie, so here he had invented ambient video, slow-moving, restful images that, combined with his music, would create a sense of gentle stasis. These videos were exhibited at galleries the following year under the title *Mistaken Memories of Mediaeval Manhattan* and were eventually released on VHS in the 1980s (where you had to watch it with your TV turned sideways) and in 2005 where you had a horizontal option. Eno's notes on the DVD release explain his intentions:

I see TV as a picture medium rather than a narrative medium. Video, for me is a way of configuring light, just as painting is a way of configuring paint. What you see is simply light patterned in various ways. For an artist, video is the best light organ that anyone has ever invented.

In reality, though Eno had gone back to his university days and become a visual artist once again, where his musical compositions almost played a secondary role to that of the visuals.

It would be two musical projects that immersed Eno in studio time for the rest of 1979 and helped him bridge the gap of the decade that loomed before him.

In August, Talking Heads' *Fear Of Music* album was released to rave reviews all round, and suddenly Eno was in vogue again with reviewers who had written him off because of *Lodger*. The reviews were hyperbolic, stating that Eno's production work and obvious experimentation had helped lift an already high-quality set of songs even higher. *Lodger* was now seen as the one mistake that all artists were allowed to make and suddenly, after months of being a music paper pariah, Eno was back in their good books, with some referring to him as 'the fifth Head'.

After the tour in support of the album, Byrne would meet up with both Eno and Hassell to discuss the possibilities of expanding 'fourth world' music. The trio would mull over such artists as the Eno-produced Penguin Cafe Orchestra and a recent album by art-rock weirdos The Residents that miked purely synthetic sounds to create an imaginary musical for Eskimos as well as the Krautrock band Can, who had begun to make inroads in a similar direction. Eno and Byrne decided that they wanted to explore this area further and make an album using the style of music as a launch pad, little realising at the time how influential the record would become.

Before these recordings could take place, Eno headed to Ontario in Canada to the studio of Bob and Daniel Lanois called Grant Studios. This studio was much cheaper than anywhere in New York, and it was here that Eno began work on an album with Harold Budd, this time not just a producer as on Budd's Obscure album, but as a co-writer and performer. The Lanois brothers were also friends with a guitar player called Michael Brook, who also played an important part in Eno's recording career in the next couple of years.

Rather than the African and world music rhythms that were flooding Eno's brain in the US, the music produced in Canada would have a sublime sense of stillness to it, the most opposite sound compared to what Eno had been currently working on for most of the year. Budd had already started work on the album, mailing Eno tapes of pieces he had already written, such as 'Not Yet Remembered', and the album was definitely thought of as being a two-way collaboration, although Eno was squeezing his commitment in during his spare time until the two finally got together at the Lanois studio. *Pavilion Of Dreams* had had some of the most favourable reviews of all the Obscure releases and was the beginning of Budd making a name for himself internationally, so it was understandable why he wanted to work with Eno, who had helped to give him his first flush of success. The two men worked in a similar way to the recording pattern that Eno undertook with Fripp, with Eno laying down atmospherics and sounds for Budd to perform over. Occasionally Eno added extra instrumentation, and of course, he would be treating Budd's piano playing as well, but the melodies mainly came from Budd, who was playing amongst the sound world that Eno had created for him. This wasn't a necessary form of improvisation as some of the pieces were already written but were altered by Budd, as Eno explained; 'His way of composing was to write a piece of music, then take out all the notes you didn't like!'

The music produced was serene and beautiful and drifted like a summer stream through the speakers. Budd's acoustic and electric piano études shimmered against Eno's slowly drifting backing. Obviously, at some point, Eno had convinced Budd that this would be the perfect second album for his Ambient label imprint as it certainly kept a flavour, if not the high concept idea, of the previous release. The record was finally released in April 1980 under the title *Ambient 2: The Plateaux Of Mirror* and was adorned with a variation of the cover that had been on *Music For Airports*. When Budd and Hassell's records were finally released, the *NME*, which was going through 'if it's not ska music, it is not worth listening to' period, lambasted the albums as being pro-Thatcherite muzak against the latest fad's political message. In July of 1980, Eno did an interview for Cynthia Rose of *NME* where he hit back at criticisms of the two albums:

I was thinking about this the other day – Actually, I was responding to the review in NME of the Harold Budd and Jon Hassell records I've just done, and I was thinking, why does this piss me off?' It didn't piss me off a lot, but before those records were released, I wrote what I thought was a mock-NME review as a joke while I was talking to Harold. Some of it I got word for word, and I thought, 'Fuck me! I've been away from this country for two years and I can still make accurate predictions about what's going to happen on the 'fashionable' level. I thought, well, it's not interesting, and then thought again, well, why isn't it interesting? And decided what I thought had happened is that all the papers have got involved in a fairly local ideological struggle. They've all taken new wave and punk much more seriously than any musicians I know. For the musicians, it was not even a defined term as such. No one who was working in that area saw such clear boundaries and definitions and meanings as writers have. And it seems to me now they have made such a heavy emotional investment that they have to put a lot of distance between themselves and anything which does not fit into a certain area – as those two records obviously don't.

By late 1979 Eno was back in New York and back in the studio to rapidly record what would be the third volume of his Ambient imprint releases, Laraaji's *Day Of Radiance* album, which would bear the legend 'Produced by Brian Eno' on its front cover. The album was a suite of hammered dulcimer pieces that crossed between rhythmic Gamelan-style tracks and those that were more meditative. Eno covered the proceedings with washes of reverb and echo to make it sound as if Laraaji was playing in some vast cavern (something he would do on one of his later albums *Flow Goes The Universe*), and although the record is not as drifting as the previous two releases, it certainly stands up well on its own even if it does stick out like a sore thumb among the other Ambient releases; the cover again uniformly fitted with that of *Music For Airports* and the notes about the recording were minimal, in fact most of the back cover is a large white space. It is perhaps the most obscure of the four releases and the one that certainly sold less than the other three when it was released the following year. It was the album that almost disappeared from the catalogue until it had a recent reissue, finally doing the record some justice. It would though launch Laraaji's career that has seen him record dozens of albums.

This was the last recording that Eno was involved with in the seventies, a decade that had seen him touch upon and transform many areas of rock music in just eight short years. On New Year's Eve, Eno flew to California for a break and to recharge his batteries, no doubt looking back at his achievements over the past decade and wondering what the new one would hold for him. He had gone from glam rock poseur to serious rock academic in a short space of time and everybody had just seemed to accept that this had happened without questioning it. Unlike other glam rock stars, he had managed to shake off the image fairly easily without being criticised for it or it being used against him like other early seventies glam stars. The Brian Eno who entered the eighties was an unrecognisable one from the Eno who had entered the seventies. The seventies had given him a platform to grow in different directions and armed with this, he entered the new decade full of confidence and with a critically acclaimed and eclectic body of work behind him.

Afterword: Eno In The Eighties And Beyond

The eighties would come to define what Eno is for the rest of his career. He became the architect of sound; the producer that gave bands their biggest hits and the quiet, introspective thinker and creator of ambient music. Eno also branched more into visual arts at this point, not only with his video work, but also by the mid-eighties, the sound and light installations that he would travel the world with, creating an almost concert experience for his fans, as he himself would very rarely play live.

During the early eighties, Eno was often claimed as an influence by artists on the new romantic/futurist scene that was producing huge hit singles at this point, and this meant that many people would go and investigate his back catalogue of works, such as bands like Duran Duran and Japan, and then wax lyrical about him.

However, Eno's decade didn't start well. In January, he received the news that Peter Schmidt had died from a heart attack. Eno had lost his long-time artistic collaborator, the only artist (bar Fripp) who had helped him weather the storm of his post-Roxy career throughout the seventies and be his collaborator on the now-famous Oblique Strategies. Eno would be part of, and help organise, an exhibition of Schmidt's work in France, making available for the first time many ideas and pieces they had worked on together.

Eno now turned to Yorkshire-born artist Russell Mills to help design many of the releases he was now involved in putting out via EG Records. Mills helped create the aesthetic look for ambient music in the early eighties and worked with many musicians connected with Eno and some who were on the periphery, such as David Sylvian (who was going to work with Eno in the mid-eighties but neither could agree on ideas). Mills also collaborated on exhibitions and became one of the better-known visual (and music) artists associated with Eno. Between 1986 and 1989, Mills ran an intermittent ambient music night in St Peter's Church, Vauxhall, London, where many artists, including Eno, performed live, some for the first time in many years. In 1980, Eno and Mills appeared in a BBC *Arena* documentary together under the title *Double Vision* – discussions here included Eno's influence on Mills's work.

Eno's first releases were those records he had worked on at the end of 1979, the two albums of his Ambient label and the one with Hassell. It wasn't until 1981 that the fruits of his collaboration with Byrne were released, with some of the backing material dating to the initial sessions back in 1979. This was also Eno's only solo/collaborative work released that year, and it is certainly a record that sets itself apart musically more than anything else Eno released for the next five years. In 1979 Eno was selling the idea of the album to Byrne by saying that it would be part of a library series of records using the 'ethno-geographical' sound. Eno was always one for having albums come in groups of sounds. Originally Jon Hassell was to be involved and was invited along to initial sessions for the album, but in the end, Hassell declined to be involved in the project and Eno's new series of albums would only bear one fruit which would be *My Life In The Bush Of Ghosts*. As in the usual Eno style, the recording were experimental and somewhat ad hoc as well, with musicians finding any objects lying around the studio to hit to make percussive sounds that are the cornerstone of the album; these instruments included ashtrays, plastic rubbish bins and lampshades etc. The cut and paste voices were already beginning to be an up-and-coming thing with a couple of artists already beginning to use it, including British band Cabaret Voltaire, but it was Eno and Byrne that birthed the true monster of an album made totally of found voices. Even though the album was completed in 1980, getting the authorisation to use the appropriated vocal performances was lengthy and time-consuming, meaning that the album was not released until 1981, and even when it was, a track called 'Qu'ran' had to be removed from further pressings of the record due to a complaint from the British-based World Council of Islam, so only first pressings contain this track.

It was also around this point that Eno began to work with his younger brother Roger. Unlike his older sibling, Roger had studied music at the Colchester Institute from age 16 so he certainly was not the avowed 'non-musician' that Eno had always claimed to be and is mostly known as a pianist even though he is a multi-instrumentalist. Their first work together, with Daniel Lanois, was the haunting soundtrack to the 1989 film about the NASA moon landings called *For All Mankind*. Even though this music was recorded and released in 1983 under the title *Apollo: Atmospheres and Soundtracks* it would take a further six years for the movie to have its premiere. This confused many Eno fans who were searching for the film discussed on the notes on the reverse side of the album sleeve, only to have to wait all that time to finally see both music and images together. In 1985 Eno produced Roger's Satie-like melancholy études for his first solo album called *Voices* which was also released through EG records. Roger has released over 30 albums working with people such as Laraaji and Peter Hammill. In 2020 the Eno brothers released their first joint collaboration, a double album with the title *Mixing Colours* which led to them doing a one-off live performance at the Acropolis in Greece, which is rumoured to be getting a Blu-ray/DVD release, as it was professionally filmed and excerpts keep being leaked to YouTube.

In 1982 Eno released what would be the final part of his 'Ambient' imprint. *On Land*, its title slightly appropriated from a short film by surrealist filmmaker Maya Deren, had the prefix 'Ambient 4'. The album was a very different beast than the previous releases using more deep bass throbs and hanging atmospheres and forsaking any real melodies in favour of an almost ambient drone that carried over from track to track. The location names used as some of the track titles would mainly be of local places that Eno visited when he was growing up. The atmosphere of the album does permeate with an essence of memory and so could be conceived as Eno's most personal album to date. The album was recorded over a three-year period at different studios, including Eno's old perennial Basing Street as well as the Lanois Studio in Canada. Eno referred to the album as 'a nice kind of spooky'; because of the protracted nature of the recordings, they merge together in their melancholy very well. Steven Grant, in *Trouser Press* magazine in August 1982, asked Eno about his new way of composing:

I'm always starting pieces of work. It's the only thing I do, really, these pieces don't go anywhere. For some reason, one of them will touch something in me. I never understand why at the time. As soon as I've got that, I recognise it as being the seed for something. There follows a period of looking at it in different ways, putting things with it, seeing how it reacts with other things – as you might do a chemical. The breakthrough stage is when I suddenly get a strong sense of mood or place. It's like a foetal idea at the time. I have to surround it with things that will nourish it, if you like, that's when I start thinking about psychoacoustics and electronics. Then craft enters into it.

Eno, in the same interview, would discuss ambient music and its meaning by saying:

I like it as an ambiguous term. It gives me a certain latitude. 'On Land' (is) creating an ambience, a sense of place that complements and alters your environment. Both meanings are contained in the word ambient.

Eno's main idea now was to create a type of ambient mush so that listeners wouldn't be able to pick out the kind of instruments used within a piece. It also meant that the listener would be unaware of the kind of thought process and playing techniques deployed, thus making it easier for other artists to layer their own productions over Eno's own composition. as It would have a similar type of background noise as waves breaking on a beach, both noticeable, and after a while, ignorable as well. For the first time ever though, Eno's titles and music hinted at a virtual geography and an endless interior space in the places they wanted to conjure up in the listener's imagination. However, the track 'Tal Coat' was a direct reference to the French 1930s artist Pierre Tal-Coat, who was one of the founder members of Tachisme, a form of abstract art that was not too dissimilar to the kind of work that was now adorning Eno's album sleeves. *On Land* included the obligatory guest musicians such as Bill Laswell, Axel Gros, Michael Brook and Jon Hassell, but these contributions were muted in the mush of the overall sound so that in some places, they are barely discernible in the wash of the overall atmosphere.

It was during this time that Eno patented a three-way speaker system for home music centres which gave the optimum sound for playback for the album. A diagram of how this could be set up was shown on the reverse of the album sleeve under the title 'The Ambient Speaker System', so how many Enophiles tried to rig up this playback feature is anyone's guess. *On Land* marked another ending for Eno as he now embarked on making the kind of low-event horizon music he wanted to without having to categorise for the public or even for reviewers. His next three releases were all collaborations and it would be three years until the next Eno proper solo release.

1983 saw the release of one of Eno's most important collaborative projects of the eighties, and *Apollo: Atmospheres and Soundtracks* is now widely regarded as one of Eno's high-water marks from this era. One of the tracks solely composed and played by Eno called 'An Ending' has been used copious times for adverts and various documentaries, removing it now almost totally from what the piece was originally composed for, which of course, was Al Reinert's film. The album itself mixes country music-style pedal steel guitar-playing numbers with those that are heavy on atmospherics and Tangerine Dream-style cosmic soundscapes. The album drifts in the upper atmosphere and was apparently a favourite music to listen to for astronomers at one point. Eno's instrument of choice for the album was the newly released and newly bought by Eno, Yamaha DX7, a digital synth, sounds from which was eventually used extensively in adverts in the UK. Eno, of course, ignored the pre-set sounds and their rather crisp sterile nature to dive deep into the machine and pull out some very Eno sounds from it, making it, of course, not sound like a DX7. The album again was recorded at the Lanois studio late in 1982 and was released in July 1983 with a rare Eno single of the track 'Deep Blue Day' preceding it. The track appeared on the soundtrack to Mark Romanek's 1985 film *Static*, a full four years before it graced the visuals it was originally composed for. Some of the Apollo pieces appeared on *Music For Films Vol 2,* which also appeared in 1983 and collected together some of Eno's more recent film score work. Also compiled the same year was a nine-album box set retrospective of all of Eno's albums under the title *Working Backwards 1983–1973*, and this also featured a 12" of 'Rarities' that included 'Seven Deadly Finns', 'The Lion Sleeps Tonight (Wimoweh)' and three previously unreleased instrumentals 'Strong Flashes Of Light', 'More Volts' and 'Mist/Rhythm'. Some record shops broke up these box sets and sold the discs individually, including the 12", but you can still recognise these pressings as they have a gold stamp mark of 'EG Box' on them.

The next two titles Eno was involved with were a collaboration with Harold Budd called *The Pearl* and Michael Brook's first solo album/ collaboration called *Hybrid*. *The Pearl* drifts through a series of delicate and melancholy piano pieces all constructed by Budd, where Eno added his usual atmospherics and treatments. The record sounds beautifully autumnal as the slow Satie-like pieces drift around the room, giving an air of contemplation hanging in the atmosphere. Brook's album is an odd cross-pollination between *On Land* and *Possible Musics,* sometimes using ethnic rhythms but always everything swathed in Eno's treatments and keyboard playing. Sadly, the album is now slightly overlooked and has been out of print on all formats for many years, but the album has many merits and really should warrant a proper re-release at some point. The covers for both albums were painted and designed by Russell Mills, making them feel like they were part of a larger ambient catalogue and community.

In 1985 Eno was still trying to stay ahead and embrace the new technologies in music. The rise of the CD had started a couple of years earlier and it was growing apace. Soon CDs made old vinyl records obsolete as they began to assume control over the market. Vinyl could only store 40 minutes of music in total before sound quality was dramatically altered. For CD, the length of running time could be up to 74 minutes. Seeing this as a challenge, Eno decided he was going to record a piece of music specifically for the CD format; most compact discs so far had been digitalised reissues of existing records. It was Eno who released the first 61-minute piece of music specially composed for the format. Using the same team of Brook and Lanois, *Thursday Afternoon* ushered in the extended album format. The piece drifts along for its hour, changing imperceptibly as it goes along with a piano, playing around the chord of G. Much fuss was made about this breakthrough, especially in magazines like *Electronics & Music Maker*, and *Electronic Soundmaker & Computer Music*, who were pushing this new format as the way ahead for releases.

However, *Thursday Afternoon* also had another purpose, and this was that it was also written to accompany a series of seven video paintings that Eno had been commissioned to make by Sony Video Japan of actress and photographer Christine Alcino in early 1984, which had a running time of 84 minutes. The images were mainly distorted and over-colourised footage of Alcino in a bath or drying herself slowly with a towel. This footage was slowed down to such a degree that images acted more like paintings rather than conventional music videos. The film was finally released on a vertical format on VHS in the UK and Japan in the following year and finally had a limited DVD release in 2006 under the title *14 Video Paintings*.

However, by 1985 Eno was probably best known to most of the world as the producer of U2's multimillion-selling album *The Unforgettable Fire*. Eno and Lanois co-produced the record as Eno himself was hesitant about working with the band, even after they did a lot of grovelling to him to do it. Even Island Records, U2's label as well, were reluctant to let Eno behind the control desk, fearing that he might turn them into an 'art rock' band. Lanois were there for insurance reasons, really, so that if Eno didn't like the music, he could walk and leave the band in the trusty hands of Lanois. In the end, Eno gave them a massive reverb and echo desert guitar sound that spoke volumes to music lovers in the United States and propelled the band into a stadium rock act that they are still reaping the rewards of today. The album produced three hit singles and Eno worked with them as producer on their even bigger follow-up album *The Joshua Tree*. Eno had now become a producer in demand because of his association with these albums and soon, other more pop-orientated acts like James came knocking at Eno's door, hoping his magic behind the console would give them top-selling albums. For many Enophiles, his work with U2 was a bit of a mystery (as it would be with Coldplay in recent years) as they seemed an odd choice for him to produce. Up until this point, the artists he had produced had all come with art-house credentials that made them obvious choices for his way of working. Even stranger was the fact that Eno had turned down other popular music artists such as XTC, who were far more on the art rock spectrum than U2.

In 1986, Faber & Faber Books published the first joint Eno and Russell Mills project away from album covers. Mills had been working on paintings for some years depicting Eno's lyrics in a visual form. The book compiled all these paintings together along with text by Mills on the creative process, and essays by Eno and Rick Poynter and discussions about the meaning of the words as well as about ambient music. The book, called *More Dark Than Shark*, also spawned a compilation album of vocal songs by Eno called *More Blank Than Frank,* with initial copies including a free Mills print of one of his paintings. This was Eno's final record release as a performer for the rest of the eighties, as fans would have to wait four years for his collaboration album with John Cale called *Wrong Way Up*.

Apart from sitting in the producer's chair, Eno's time and energy and thought process was to be taken with the staging of sound and light installation exhibitions in various cities around the world. The first of these was in Frankfurt in Germany and Rome in Italy. The exhibitions were a totally immersive experience as you entered a pitch-black room only lit up by Eno's light sculptures and video paintings. These changed colour and movement slowly as you walked and sat within the same space as them. Each was separated into different rooms, meaning each space had its own very distinct atmosphere.

All the while, Eno's music played on a slowly evolving continuous loop that gave a sense of stillness to proceedings. Much of this music went unreleased for 33 years until they were released as a box set in 2018 under the title *Music For Installations*. Eno discussed the music with Mark Prendergast in 1989 in the January issue of *Sound On Sound* magazine:

The music in these installations repeats over a very, very, long time cycle; for example, 60 weeks or 100 weeks. These are very, very long pieces of music, and they are made long by allowing several cycles to constantly run out of sync with each other. The technical problem involved was trying to make a piece of music which I would never hear and could never predict. Obviously, I have never heard this piece of music properly – maybe only for 300 hours, but that is only perhaps three percent of its life.

All my work aspires to the condition of painting. What I like about painters is that they stay there, they persist. I like to see a painting on the wall, and I like to look at it. I can stay for as long as I want and then get on with what I am doing, then I can go back to that again and then get on with what I am doing again. So, I want to make music that has that condition of being almost static but not completely so.

Some critics have thought that Eno's video paintings bear a resemblance to the work of artist Wassily Kandinsky because of the similarity between shapes and colours that the artist used. A book about Eno's exhibitions and their history called *Brian Eno Visual Music* was published in 2019.

The other thing that was taking up Eno's time was the forming of 'Opal Ltd' with EG company director and Eno's then-partner, now wife Anthea Norman-Taylor. Opal released albums and took under its wing several artists such as Harold Budd and Jon Hassell, who had worked with Eno and pulled in some that hadn't. This was also somewhat of a problem as when it got around that Eno now had his own label (Opal Records), the offices were inundated with tapes from hundreds of artists creating a form of ambient or New Age music wanting to be released by the label and hoping the association with Eno would help to kick-start their careers. In fact, the first four releases by Opal were by Roger Eno (*Between Tides*), Harold Budd (*The White Arcades*), Hugo Largo (*Drum*) and *Music For Films 3*. These were on Opal's imprint 'Land Records', which lasted approximately two years, but over time the label name was finally changed to 'All Saints' and took on a slightly more diverse range of artists. Opal also ran occasional evenings at the Queen Elizabeth Hall in London, but these mainly consisted of tried and tested artists such as Harold Budd and Roger Eno.

As Eno moved into the nineties, his first release was with Cale, but their working relationship during the making of the record slowly deteriorated. The making of the album seemed fraught with arguments, and after what was a beginning filled with camaraderie, the two men slowly fell out as the recordings progressed. His other major collaboration of the nineties was with former PIL bassist Jah Wobble. *Spinner*, released in 1995, was an odd amalgamation of sounds and styles that slightly jarred with each other, and Wobble only seems to actually appear on six of the album's ten tracks.

In 1993, Philip Glass had written a symphony based on the *Low* album and the work initially only had Bowie's name attached to it, so Glass had to be gently reminded that some of the compositions he was using were co-writes (or in Warszawa's case totally written) by Eno. The record was a great success and in the intervening years, Glass has also written symphonies to both *Heroes* (1997) and, more recently, *Lodger* as well, making sure Eno's name is fully intact in the publicity associated with them.

Eno ploughed a furrow with his own releases, sometimes drawing from music recorded earlier from his vast archive. However, 1992's *Nerve Net* broke the ambient mould with Eno returning briefly to more rock-orientated tracks that mixed jazz style playing with electronics. It is seen as quite a dark album for Eno as well as the solo album with the largest amount of guest musicians playing on it. *The Shutov Assembly*, also 1992, and *Neroli (Thinking Music Part 4)* (1993) were far more standard Eno ambient fare, moving the sound ever slightly forward incrementally. In 1997, *Music For White Cube* was a limited release CD of pieces written especially for a sound installation Eno gave at London's White Cube gallery, which consisted of four CD players playing tracks of Brian singing one note with background traffic and street sounds which had been slowed down; the CDs would probably slightly fall out of sync with each other, which was Eno echoing the work of his minimalist heroes.

In 1995 Eno and Bowie worked together once again on the much underrated *1. Outside (The Nathan Adler Diaries: A Hyper Cycle)*. The pair had patched up any differences they had during the final stages of *Lodger* and seemed to enjoy working with each other again, with the pressure finally off, both men were eager to be at the cutting edge of music-making.

For a man who often quoted that he never liked to look back on himself or do situations that he had done before, Eno had already revisited his past with Bowie, and during the 2000s, he would do the same with Fripp for the 2004 release *The Equatorial Stars* and with David Byrne on 2008's *Everything That Happens Will Happen Today*. Other collaborations came in the form of 2001's *Drawn From Life* with J Peter Schwalm and Michel Faber for 2005's *The Fahrenheit Twins*. But it was with 2005's solo album *Another Day On Earth* that Eno probably made his best vocal songs since *Before And After Science*, this time with a minimum of guest artists appearing on the record. Eno songs twinkle like distant stars or shimmer like a heat haze throughout the course of its 11 songs.

Much of Eno's subsequent work over the last 12 years has followed a similar path to that which he carved out for himself in the 1980s, a mixture of the odd vocal album like 2015's *My Squelchy Life* mixed with collaborations such as 2011's release with Rick Holland called *Drums Between The Bells* and his usual ambient pieces such as the contemplative *Lux* from 2012, whose four pieces add a sense of stillness to any room it's playing in; also 2017's *Reflection* that picks a similar path to that of *Lux*. To some, this might seem like an element of stasis in Eno's work, but after 50 years as a recording artist, I think this can be allowed. Interest in his work probably comes mainly from his hard-core fan base, which, if social media pages are true, runs into quite a few thousand people.

Eno has always played around with as many mediums as possible at the same time, so as well as the exhibitions, he has had a couple of books published, the most famous of these being his 1996 volume *A Year With Swollen Appendices*, a diary which he had kept during the year 1995, and a book that became infamous for an entry Eno made about drinking his own urine. In 2020 an updated version of this was released for its 25th anniversary with a new introduction and notes by Eno.

There was, of course, also the failed Roxy Music reunion, whose recordings have so far never been released, even though both Manzanera and Mackay have said in interviews that they wish they would be. The master tapes seem to be held by Ferry, who was meant to add vocals to them but whose lyric writing muse seems to have left him briefly. Eno was going to do the tour with the band, but only if they played some new material. With the album unfinished, the tour went ahead with the band focusing on early Roxy classics but without Eno on stage behind his trusty VCS3. In a strange way, it is the biggest missed opportunity in rock music but might also be seen as Eno's get-out-of-jail clause about doing a lengthy tour as he seemed to have doubts at the start of the reunion whether Ferry would ever complete the recordings. In 2023, it will be the fiftieth anniversary of *For Your Pleasure* and also 50 years since Eno last stepped onstage with Roxy, so it would be a wonderful thing to see them play together one more time to celebrate this milestone, but one doubts that this would ever seriously happen. Hopefully, Eno will decide to play more than one-off live events again at some point (2021 saw him play live with Roger and it would be wonderful if this would happen again at other locations).

It's difficult to predict exactly where Eno will go next with his art: musically, we can probably expect more ambient albums of a similar nature to *Lux*; visually, he seems to be broadening his palette as a recent projection onto the Sydney Opera House in Australia has shown. We can certainly expect more collaborations like the recent *Dokument #2* in 2020 with Laurie Anderson and, of course, more soundtracks like 2020's *Rams* from the documentary of the same name. It has now been well over ten years since his last collaborations with either Byrne or Fripp, so I doubt that these are on his radar anytime soon, and sadly the passing of Harold Budd in 2020 means there will be no further projects from him. In recent years Eno has become more politically vocal, something he said he would never do in the seventies, and he even gave out flyers for the last UK general election for the Labour Party.

For many of his fans, his seventies output is still seen as his high-water mark musically, where he seemed to constantly be ahead of the curve and sometimes at a place all of his own making. The body of work he made during this period was full of 'Enovations' and had a constant forward momentum about it that within the space of two years, his sound was barely recognisable from records he was making before. For many, like myself, seeing Eno on pop music television programmes in the early seventies with Roxy Music was a kick-starter to try and find out more about this alien creature and the strange instrument he appeared to be 'playing'. The seventies were when Brian Eno helped to change the course of rock music forever and inspired many musicians to start looking at their work in the broader spectrum of art.

My interest in making music has been to create something that does not exist that I would like to listen to. I wanted to hear music that had not yet happened by putting together things that suggested a new thing which did not yet exist.
Brian Eno.

On Track series

Alan Parsons Project – Steve Swift
978-1-78952-154-2
Tori Amos – Lisa Torem 978-1-78952-142-9
Asia – Peter Braidis 978-1-78952-099-6
Badfinger – Robert Day-Webb
978-1-878952-176-4
Barclay James Harvest – Keith and Monica Domone
978-1-78952-067-5
The Beatles – Andrew Wild 978-1-78952-009-5
The Beatles Solo 1969-1980 – Andrew Wild
978-1-78952-030-9
Blue Oyster Cult – Jacob Holm-Lupo
978-1-78952-007-1
Blur – Matt Bishop 978-178952-164-1
Marc Bolan and T.Rex – Peter Gallagher
978-1-78952-124-5
Kate Bush – Bill Thomas 978-1-78952-097-2
Camel – Hamish Kuzminski 978-1-78952-040-8
Caravan – Andy Boot 978-1-78952-127-6
Cardiacs – Eric Benac 978-1-78952-131-3
Eric Clapton Solo – Andrew Wild
978-1-78952-141-2
The Clash – Nick Assirati 978-1-78952-077-4
Crosby, Stills and Nash – Andrew Wild
978-1-78952-039-2
The Damned – Morgan Brown
978-1-78952-136-8
Deep Purple and Rainbow 1968-79 –
Steve Pilkington 978-1-78952-002-6
Dire Straits – Andrew Wild 978-1-78952-044-6
The Doors – Tony Thompson
978-1-78952-137-5
Dream Theater – Jordan Blum
978-1-78952-050-7
Electric Light Orchestra – Barry Delve
978-1-78952-152-8
Elvis Costello and The Attractions –
Georg Purvis 978-1-78952-129-0
Emerson Lake and Palmer – Mike Goode
978-1-78952-000-2
Fairport Convention – Kevan Furbank
978-1-78952-051-4
Peter Gabriel – Graeme Scarfe
978-1-78952-138-2
Genesis – Stuart MacFarlane 978-1-78952-005-7
Gentle Giant – Gary Steel 978-1-78952-058-3
Gong – Kevan Furbank 978-1-78952-082-8
Hall and Oates – Ian Abrahams
978-1-78952-167-2
Hawkwind – Duncan Harris 978-1-78952-052-1
Peter Hammill – Richard Rees Jones
978-1-78952-163-4
Roy Harper – Opher Goodwin 978-1-78952-130-6
Jimi Hendrix – Emma Stott 978-1-78952-175-7
The Hollies – Andrew Darlington
978-1-78952-159-7
Iron Maiden – Steve Pilkington
978-1-78952-061-3

Jefferson Airplane – Richard Butterworth
978-1-78952-143-6
Jethro Tull – Jordan Blum 978-1-78952-016-3
Elton John in the 1970s – Peter Kearns
978-1-78952-034-7
The Incredible String Band – Tim Moon
978-1-78952-107-8
Iron Maiden – Steve Pilkington
978-1-78952-061-3
Judas Priest – John Tucker 978-1-78952-018-7
Kansas – Kevin Cummings 978-1-78952-057-6
The Kinks – Martin Hutchinson
978-1-78952-172-6
Korn – Matt Karpe 978-1-78952-153-5
Led Zeppelin – Steve Pilkington
978-1-78952-151-1
Level 42 – Matt Philips 978-1-78952-102-3
Little Feat – 978-1-78952-168-9
Aimee Mann – Jez Rowden 978-1-78952-036-1
Joni Mitchell – Peter Kearns 978-1-78952-081-1
The Moody Blues – Geoffrey Feakes
978-1-78952-042-2
Motorhead – Duncan Harris 978-1-78952-173-3
Mike Oldfield – Ryan Yard 978-1-78952-060-6
Opeth – Jordan Blum 978-1-78-952-166-5
Tom Petty – Richard James 978-1-78952-128-3
Porcupine Tree – Nick Holmes
978-1-78952-144-3
Queen – Andrew Wild 978-1-78952-003-3
Radiohead – William Allen 978-1-78952-149-8
Renaissance – David Detmer 978-1-78952-062-0
The Rolling Stones 1963-80 – Steve Pilkington 978-1-78952-017-0
The Smiths and Morrissey –
Tommy Gunnarsson 978-1-78952-140-5
Status Quo the Frantic Four Years –
Richard James 978-1-78952-160-3
Steely Dan – Jez Rowden 978-1-78952-043-9
Steve Hackett – Geoffrey Feakes
978-1-78952-098-9
Thin Lizzy – Graeme Stroud 978-1-78952-064-4
Toto – Jacob Holm-Lupo 978-1-78952-019-4
U2 – Eoghan Lyng 978-1-78952-078-1
UFO – Richard James 978-1-78952-073-6
The Who – Geoffrey Feakes
978-1-78952-076-7
Roy Wood and the Move – James R Turner
978-1-78952-008-8
Van Der Graaf Generator – Dan Coffey
978-1-78952-031-6
Yes – Stephen Lambe 978-1-78952-001-9
Frank Zappa 1966 to 1979 – Eric Benac
978-1-78952-033-0
Warren Zevon – Peter Gallagher
978-1-78952-170-2
10CC – Peter Kearns 978-1-78952-054-5

and many more to come!